Biography Today

**Profiles
of People
of Interest
to Young
Readers**

Volume 16
Issue 1
January 2007

Cherie D. Abbey
Managing Editor

Omnigraphics

*615 Griswold Street
Detroit, Michigan 48226*

Cherie D. Abbey, *Managing Editor*

Kevin Hillstrom, *Editor*

Joan Axelrod-Contrada, Peggy Daniels, Laurie DiMauro, Sheila Fitzgerald,
Joan Goldsworthy, Margaret Haerens, Leslie Karr, Eve Nagler, Sara Pendergast,
Tom Pendergast, and Diane Telgen, *Sketch Writers*

Allison A. Beckett, Mary Butler, and Linda Strand, *Research Staff*

* * *

Peter E. Ruffner, *Publisher*
Frederick G. Ruffner, Jr., *Chairman*
Matthew P. Barbour, *Senior Vice President*
Kay Gill, *Vice President — Directories*

* * *

David P. Bianco, *Marketing Director*
Elizabeth Collins, *Research and Permissions Coordinator*
Kevin Hayes, *Operations Manager*
Barry Puckett, *Librarian*
Cherry Stockdale, *Permissions Assistant*

Shirley Amore, Martha Johns, Kirk Kauffman,
and Johnny Lawrence, *Administrative Staff*

This book is printed on acid-free paper meeting the ANSI Z39.48 Standard. The infini-
ty symbol that appears above indicates that the paper in this book meets that standard.

Printed in the United States

Contents

Preface

Biography Today is a magazine designed and written for the young reader — ages 9 and above — and covers individuals that librarians and teachers tell us that young people want to know about most: entertainers, athletes, writers, illustrators, cartoonists, and political leaders.

The Plan of the Work

The publication was especially created to appeal to young readers in a format they can enjoy reading and readily understand. Each issue contains approximately 10 sketches arranged alphabetically. Each entry provides at least one picture of the individual profiled, and bold-faced rubrics lead the reader to information on birth, youth, early memories, education, first jobs, marriage and family, career highlights, memorable experiences, hobbies, and honors and awards. Each of the entries ends with a list of easily accessible sources designed to lead the student to further reading on the individual and a current address. Retrospective entries are also included, written to provide a perspective on the individual's entire career.

Biographies are prepared by Omnigraphics editors after extensive research, utilizing the most current materials available. Those sources that are generally available to students appear in the list of further reading at the end of the sketch.

Indexes

Cumulative indexes are an important component of *Biography Today*. Each issue of the *Biography Today* General Series includes a Cumulative Names Index, which comprises all individuals profiled in *Biography Today* since the series began in 1992. In addition, we compile three other indexes: the Cumulative General Index, Places of Birth Index, and Birthday Index. See our web site, www.biographytoday.com, for these three indexes, along with the Names Index. All *Biography Today* indexes are cumulative, including all individuals profiled in both the General Series and the Subject Series.

Our Advisors

This series was reviewed by an Advisory Board comprised of librarians, children's literature specialists, and reading instructors to ensure that the concept of this publication — to provide a readable and accessible biographical magazine for young readers — was on target. They evaluated the title as it developed, and their suggestions have proved invaluable. Any errors, however, are ours alone. We'd like to list the Advisory Board members, and to thank them for their efforts.

Our Advisory Board stressed to us that we should not shy away from controversial or unconventional people in our profiles, and we have tried to follow their advice. The Advisory Board also mentioned that the sketches might be useful in reluctant reader and adult literacy programs, and we would value any comments librarians might have about the suitability of our magazine for those purposes.

Your Comments Are Welcome

Our goal is to be accurate and up-to-date, to give young readers information they can learn from and enjoy. Now we want to know what you think. Take a look at this issue of *Biography Today*, on approval. Write or call me with your comments. We want to provide an excellent source of biographical information for young people. Let us know how you think we're doing.

Cherie Abbey
Managing Editor, *Biography Today*
Omnigraphics, Inc.
615 Griswold Street
Detroit, MI 48226

editor@biographytoday.com
www.biographytoday.com

Congratulations!

Congratulations to the following individuals and libraries, who are receiving a free copy of *Biography Today*, Vol. 16, No. 1 for suggesting people who appear in this issue:

Allentown Central Catholic, Allentown, PA
Aaron Blechert, Irondale High School Media Center, New Brighton, MN
Ellen Blumberg, Westwood High School Library, Austin, TX
Rachel Q. Davis, Thomas Memorial Library, Cape Elizabeth, ME
Carrie DeForest, Roselle Middle School Library, Roselle, IL
Noel Miranda, Sacramento, CA
Rebecca Morris, Deer Lake Middle School Library, Russellton, PA
Randy Olund, Carrington Middle School Media Center, Durham, NC
Sarah Puckett, Northville, MI
Maggie and Julia Rapai, Grosse Pointe, MI

Drake Bell 1986-

American Actor and Musician
Co-Star of the Award-Winning Nickelodeon TV
Series "Drake & Josh"

BIRTH

Jared Drake Bell was born on June 27, 1986, in Newport Beach, California. He has three brothers and a sister. Bell's parents are divorced. His father, Joe Bell, is a talent manager for young actors. His mother, Robin Bell Dodson, is a former world-champion billiards player whose life has been full of twists and turns. She learned to play pool at the age of 12 and became a professional player, but heroin addiction derailed her career for several years. A renewal of her religious faith finally helped her end her dependence on drugs and turn her life around. In both 1990 and 1991, she won the women's WPBA (World Pool-Billiards Association) world championship in billiards. In 1995 she married Roy Dodson.

YOUTH

In many ways, Bell had an unusual childhood. Instead of playing soccer or other sports after school, he spent much of his time auditioning for parts in television commercials, TV series, and movies. His father first got him into acting at the age of five, when he appeared in a commercial for Whirlpool Appliances. "I had to sit under a tree and eat a Popsicle," he recalled. "I thought, 'I could get used to this.'"

> *Bell did his first commercial at age five for Whirlpool Appliances. "I had to sit under a tree and eat a Popsicle," he recalled. "I thought, 'I could get used to this.'"*

Bell found that he enjoyed the limelight, and he spent many afternoons after school in front of the camera. In fact, he became such a familiar face at auditions that casting directors and others in the business even took to calling him "One Take Drake" for his ability to get everything right on the first try. But in other respects, his interests were those of a typical teenager. He liked listening to music, watching television, and playing video games with friends. Surprisingly, Bell never learned to play pool even though his mother was a world champion. "It's a game that can take you in the wrong direction, so my mom kinda kept us away from the table," he said.

EDUCATION

During his years at the Vineyard Christian School in Costa Mesa, California, Bell's involvement in show business greatly influenced his attitude toward school. "I didn't want to do what other kids did," he recalled. "I wanted to build my career." As a result, he got a different kind of education from most young people his age. For example, Bell's acting jobs sometimes took him to places that most young people learn about only in textbooks. "How many kids his age get to travel to Third World countries and see the poverty first-hand?" noted Joe Bell, his father and manager. "He gets an education that 90 percent of children don't get because he gets to travel. He's a better, well-rounded child for acting."

Bell attended the Orange County High School of the Arts but he freely admits he was a poor student who did not apply himself. This disinterest in traditional school, combined with his thriving career, led him to leave school and earn a GED (general equivalency diploma) instead.

CAREER HIGHLIGHTS

Hard work, talent, and perseverance helped Bell climb the career ladder from commercials to small acting parts. His acting credits during these early years ranged from small roles on popular TV shows such as "Seinfeld," "The Drew Carey Show," and "Home Improvement" to appearances alongside film stars Denis Leary and John Cusack. Bell appeared with Leary in the 1995 feature film *The Neon Bible*, a tale about a dysfunctional family in rural Georgia. He also played John Cusack's son in the 1999 HBO film *The Jack Bull* and won a small part in the 2000 feature film *High Fidelity*.

Big Break with *Jerry Maguire*

It was in the 1996 blockbuster film *Jerry Maguire*, however, that Bell truly caught Hollywood's attention. In *Jerry Maguire* Bell plays Jesse Remo, an injured hockey player's son who angrily condemns the ethics and morality of a high-powered sports agent played by Tom Cruise. In real-life, Drake was awed by Cruise, who invited him into his trailer to play video games. "I, like, couldn't believe I was with Tom Cruise," he told a reporter.

Bell's role in *Jerry Maguire* also required him to use a swear word. According to Bell's father, his ten-year-old son wrestled with his conscience about it but ultimately decided that it was his professional obligation to read the line as it was written. "That's when I realized that Drake was growing up," Joe Bell recalled

Bell's next notable feature film role was in the 2001 movie *Changing Destiny.* He learned to play guitar for the role with a helping hand from fellow cast member Roger Daltrey, the front man of the legendary 1960s band The Who. Bell promptly fell in love with the guitar, started writing songs, and formed his own rock band.

"The Amanda Show"

In 1999, the 13-year-old Bell landed a role as a regular on the Nickelodeon sketch comedy "The Amanda Show," starring Amanda Bynes. The show brought Bell together with Josh Peck, another longtime child actor. Peck and Bell had met earlier on the Nickelodeon game show "Double Dare," but they did not hit it off at first. "Our original meeting was a fiasco," Peck remembered. "It wasn't exactly love at first sight."

When the two actors were reunited on "The Amanda Show," however, Bell and Peck became friends. In addition, the show boosted both of their careers. Bell was given the opportunity to show off his guitar-playing skills as the effortlessly cool character of Totally Kyle. The heavyset Peck, in turn, unveiled a comic persona that evoked comparisons to actors such as John Candy and Jackie Gleason.

> *Bell admitted that it is not a big acting stretch for him to play the role of Drake Parker. "I guess I'm not as cool as he is, but I basically just play me." The big differences between himself and his character, he observed, are that "I'm mellower and can't fib with a straight face like Drake."*

The on-screen chemistry between Bell and Peck caught the eye of "Amanda Show" producer Dan Schneider, who had once been a child actor himself on the 1980s sitcom "Head of the Class." Within a matter of weeks, Schneider began creating a spin-off show for the two young actors.

"Drake & Josh"

On January 11, 2004, "Drake & Josh" debuted on Nickelodeon, complete with a theme song, "I Found a Way," co-written and performed by Bell. The show updates the old "odd couple" formula by pairing two high school students who have to adjust to living in the same house after Drake's mother marries Josh's father. Bell plays the cool, guitar-playing slacker who draws his dorky, responsible stepbrother into his shenanigans. The two forge a brotherly bond through their madcap adventures. A mischievous younger sister, played by Miranda Cosgrove, adds to the humorous mix.

The new show made an instant splash as Nickelodeon's highest rated season premiere in almost 10 years. "The girls are really going for Drake, who is an extremely handsome kid," Schneider observed happily. Bell, meanwhile, acknowledged that the part he plays on the show was not a big acting challenge. "I guess I'm not as cool as he is, but I basically just play me." Still, he did point out some differences between himself and his character: "I'm mellower and can't fib with a straight face like Drake Parker."

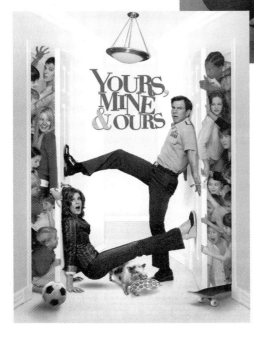

Bell in several different roles: during his days on "The Amanda Show" (top); in his bedroom on the set of "Drake & Josh" (middle); and with the cast of Yours, Mine & Ours (bottom).

Bell was delighted with the success of "Drake & Josh," but he did not let it interfere with his growing interest in music. In the fall of 2005 Bell released his first album, *Telegraph,* on the Nine Yard Records label. Bell describes his band's sound as "John Mayer meets Dave Matthews." He writes all his own songs and enjoys touring with his band. "Getting the immediate reaction from the crowd is great," he said.

The year 2005 also marked Bell's return to the big screen in the feature film *Yours, Mine & Ours,* starring Dennis Quaid and Rene Russo. Bell plays Dylan, the oldest son of an artsy mother (Russo) who enters into a second marriage with an uptight father (Quaid). The marriage brings two mismatched clans of children under the same roof. "Yeah, they're dorks in J.Crew clothes and our family is full of individuals and free spirits," Bell explained. "I'm a graffiti artist."

———— **"** ————

"The [car] accident showed me how much I love what I'm doing and that it can be taken away in a split second," Bell said.

———— **"** ————

Many critics griped that the film was bland, noisy, and predictable, but others described it as a wholesome and lighthearted family film. *Daily Variety,* for example, charged that the movie was "occasionally overzealous in hard-selling its slapstick elements." But it also commented that "*Yours, Mine & Ours* ultimately emerges as generally pleasant family-friendly fare."

Recovering from a Near-Tragedy

On December 29, 2005, Bell was seriously injured in a car accident. Another car plowed into him while he was stopped at a traffic light behind the wheel of a 1966 Ford Mustang. The Mustang did not feature a shoulder harness or airbags because such safety features did not exist in the 1960s, so Bell's injuries were quite severe. The crash fractured his neck, knocked out six teeth, and left him wondering about his future. "I was like, 'My career's over. I don't know how I'm going to look after this,'" Bell recalled.

Bell's recovery was a slow and difficult one. His jaw was wired shut for two months, which meant that smoothies became his breakfast, lunch, and dinner. "We tried putting pizza in a blender, but it smelled like vomit," he said. But friends and colleagues visited him to keep his spirits up during his convalescence. During one visit to the hospital, for instance, co-star Josh Peck told him, "You're still better looking than me, man."

Bell and Josh Peck on the set of their hit movie, Drake & Josh Go Hollywood.

Bell's spirits were also lifted by good news about the Drake & Josh television movie, *Drake & Josh Go Hollywood: The Movie,* which aired on January 6, 2006. It received the highest ratings with kids in the 6-11 and 9-14 age groups in Nickelodeon's entire broadcasting history. Some television reviewers, meanwhile, were critical of the movie's plot. But several critics commented on the on-screen chemistry between the movie's young stars.

After recuperating from his accident for a few months, Bell returned to the set of "Drake & Josh." He had a two-and-a-half-inch scar on his chin, but was happy to be back at work. "The accident showed me how much I love what I'm doing and that it can be taken away in a split second," he said.

A Fan Favorite

Bell's status as one of Hollywood's most popular young actors was confirmed on April 1, 2006, when he earned the favorite actor award at Nickelodeon's annual Kids' Choice Awards. "Drake & Josh" also took best show honors, and it rode into the fall 2006 season as television's number one-rated live-action series with kids ages 2-11. Meanwhile, plans are underway for a Drake & Josh feature film. According to *Daily Variety*, the project will "follow the well-off but sheltered Josh as he gets a crash course in life experience from popular slacker Drake."

HOME AND FAMILY

Bell lives in an apartment in Los Angeles decorated with framed Beatles posters from the 1960s. He has an extensive collection of vinyl albums, a rotary telephone, and vintage furniture and happily admits that his decorating tastes are basically "neo-grandma."

HOBBIES AND OTHER INTERESTS

Bell spends much of his spare time playing music or relaxing to music by the Beatles and other bands from the 1960s. "Nothing today compares with that music," he said. His favorite Beatle was John Lennon, but he also admires Paul McCartney and would like to someday work with him.

When he is on break from filming, Bell says that a typical day for him is to "hang out in my pajamas and eat cereal and watch cartoons." He also enjoys the work of the classic comedy duo Laurel and Hardy and 1950s movie icon James Dean. His favorite contemporary actor is Johnny Depp.

The actor/musician also makes time for charity work "to help those not as fortunate as me." For example, Bell has volunteered his time to help Gibson Musical Instruments raise money for breast cancer. "This cause hits pretty close to home," he explained. "I lost my Aunt Sandra to breast cancer."

SELECTED CREDITS

Television

"The Amanda Show," 1999-2001
"Drake & Josh," 2004-

Films

Jerry Maguire, 1996
High Fidelity, 2000
Changing Destiny, 2001
Yours, Mine & Ours, 2005
Drake & Josh Go Hollywood: The Movie, 2006 (TV movie)

Recordings

Telegraph, 2005
It's Only Time, 2006

HONORS AND AWARDS

Favorite Actor, Nickelodeon Kids Choice Awards: 2006, for "Drake & Josh"

FURTHER READING

Periodicals

Girls' Life, Feb./Mar. 2006, p.42
New York Times, Feb. 1, 2004, p.55
People, Apr. 10, 2006, p.105
Teen People, Apr. 1, 2005, p.104; Sep. 2006, p.6
TV Guide, Apr. 10, 2005, p.2

Online Articles

http://www.timeforkids.com
   (*Time for Kids*, "Chatting with Drake Bell," undated)

ADDRESS

Drake Bell
Nickelodeon Studios
231 W. Olive Ave.
Burbank, CA 91502

WORLD WIDE WEB SITES

http://www.nick.com
http://www.drakebell.com

Taylor Crabtree 1990-

American Student and Charitable Entrepreneur
Founder and Owner of TayBear Company, which
Provides Free Teddy Bears to Sick Children

EARLY YEARS

Taylor Marie Crabtree was born on September 20, 1990, in San
Diego, California. Her father, Ken Crabtree, is an engineer,
and her mother, Tricia Crabtree, is an office manager. She lives
with her parents in Rancho Santa Fe, California, not far from
San Diego. She has one older sister, Rhiannon.

An athletic girl, Crabtree was an avid gymnast when she was younger. During grade school, she also enjoyed track, tennis and swimming. Since enrolling at La Costa Canyon High School in Carlsbad, California, she has become a talented volleyball player. A straight A student, Crabtree is a member of her school's debate team and is learning American Sign Language. After graduating from high school, she hopes to attend an Ivy League college and eventually to forge a career in politics.

MAJOR ACCOMPLISHMENTS

——— *"* ———

Crabtree set a goal of providing teddy bears — "pre-hugged" by her or one of her helpers — to 50 children. "I thought her too-high goal was that of a child who didn't really understand [the challenges involved]," her mother recalled. "I was the one who didn't understand."

——— *"* ———

Crabtree first became involved in charitable activities when she was just seven years old. In October 1997 she and her mother began hand-painting hairclips for her to wear to gymnastics class. "They were so pretty I thought I could sell them," she said. Just as she was reaching that conclusion, two events increased her determination to earn money. First, her grandmother was diagnosed with colon cancer. She eventually made a full recovery, but Crabtree saw how hard it was for her to fight the disease. Crabtree then saw a TV news report about city police programs that provided teddy bears to frightened children.

These two events inspired Crabtree to comfort younger cancer patients by giving them teddy bears to hug when they were frightened or in pain. She set an initial goal of earning enough money to provide teddy bears to 50 children. "I thought her too-high goal was that of a child who didn't really understand [the challenges involved]," her mother recalled. "*I* was the one who didn't understand."

A Community Effort

Crabtree decided she would hand-paint and sell hairclips at local stores to buy bears for the children. She set up her little craft operation in her bedroom and the family kitchen, and within a matter of weeks local media outlets were publicizing the project. The growing publicity about her efforts to buy "TayBears" (a playful blend of "teddybear" and Crabtree's first name) helped get the whole community involved. Local supermarkets stuffed bags with her fliers and kept donation canisters near the checkouts, and word-of-mouth about her efforts spread through local schools and churches alike.

"Pretty soon I found out that I couldn't keep up with the inventory," Crabtree recalled. "I knew that people wanted to buy my hairclips but I was selling them faster than I could make them. I needed help fast! So I asked my friends to help and set up several 'painting parties' at my house." Eventually hundreds of other children, including special-needs children, became helpers. "Taylor wanted other kids to feel they too were capable of helping others in their own way," her mother said. "It has been rather like a chain letter from the heart."

> "When I started I didn't know anything about business," Crabtree recalled. "In school I was learning to add small numbers and stuff. That worked fine in the beginning. There were only two small numbers to add. $2.50 per hair clip times 2 makes $5, and I could add by 5s pretty well. Then the numbers started getting bigger and I learned to add bigger numbers. It happened just like that."

The project finally became so big that it outgrew the Crabtree household. The youngster promptly moved her art sessions into schools and community centers, both to accommodate her growing army of helpers and to let her mother reclaim the family kitchen for meals.

Crabtree is very proud that so many other kids have become involved in the project. In fact, only children are permitted to prepare the bears for shipping. They give each one a name, a special tag with the TayBear logo, and a big hug. "That's so they're delivered with love," Crabtree said. "By being part of TayBear, hundreds of kids have already proven that it is possible to make a difference — even if you are under five feet tall and haven't finished middle school yet."

Crabtree's efforts to get teddy bears to children who have cancer and chronic blood diseases have been heartily embraced by area hospitals, which provide her with estimates of how many children with cancer or blood diseases they see in a year. TayBear tries to provide that many bears. Crabtree visits hospitals to deliver bears in person whenever she can.

Crabtree with some of the stuffed animals collected by her organization.

Otherwise, bears are given to nurses who present the bears to young patients.

Learning about Business

Crabtree freely admits that the early days of TayBear were extremely challenging. "When I started I didn't know anything about business," she said. "In school I was learning to add small numbers and stuff. That worked fine in the beginning. There were only two small numbers to add. $2.50 per hair clip times 2 makes $5, and I could add by 5s pretty well. Then the numbers started getting bigger and I learned to add bigger numbers. It happened just like that."

Crabtree realized that she needed to know how all her money was being spent. "So I learned some Quicken [a computer-software program for business] to keep better control of my money and went to the bank to get a business account," she said. "I learned that it is hard to start a business with very little money. I started to look at my expenses in a way that I could understand. For every $5 spent . . . that would be one child without a bear."

Crabtree eagerly sought out ideas and suggestions from others to help run and improve her business. "By talking to a lot of people I'm able to get more ideas than I could have on my own. I really learned a lot about running a business," she said. She keeps careful records of all her supplies, sales donations, and of her business checking account. Crabtree also solicited companies and individuals to donate money to pay for the cost of shipping TayBears across the country. These displays of business skills have been a real eye-opener for Crabtree's mother. "I've listened with amazement as she's discussed the huggability of the teddy bears with vendors and later ordered 700 teddy bears after negotiating a lower price," she said.

Promoting TayBear

Once TayBear was firmly established, Crabtree began visiting elementary schools and middle schools across the United States to meet principals who could help her get students involved. At first, her mother went into the meetings with her. But soon she handled them on her own. "My parents have taught me that shyness doesn't get you anywhere," Crabtree said. "You just got to go for everything with all you got."

Crabtree also has shared her vision by making speeches to people — from small groups of kids to audiences of hundreds of adults. In 2000, for example, an international association of financial and insurance executives called the Million Dollar Round Table asked her to speak at its convention in San Francisco. She was their youngest-ever speaker. After asking the audience of nearly 7,000 to buy hairclips, they bought out her supply of 500 in just a few hours. The following year she received a $10,000 grant from the foundation to continue her work.

Crabtree says that another one of her most memorable speeches was delivered to the Young Entrepreneurs Organization in San Diego. Afterwards, she said, "People kept coming from the back and pulling money out, the money kept piling higher and higher on the table. My mom was crying and my dad was laughing. Here I was, just giving a normal speech and all of sudden here were all these donations." TayBear received $3,700 that day in cash gifts. Later that day, Crabtree received a promise of $10,000 from a businessman who heard her speech. The money allowed her to list her business with the U.S. government and to set up a board of directors — with herself as chairperson, president, and founder of TayBear Co.

Crabtree has continued to work on TayBear since that time. Since starting the organization in 1997, she and her hundreds of young helpers ("and a few grownups," she adds) have given away more than 20,000 bears to children in hospitals all over the United States and in Canada. "It's really kind of fun and inspiring to watch her," her father said. "She's had to cut back on some of the sports, but TayBear is another opportunity for her to develop skills other children might not and carry them into adulthood."

In January 2006, *People* magazine highlighted Crabtree and TayBear. The article featured one of the bear's recipients, a four-year-old named Andrew Granger. The little boy hugged his bear through long and difficult medical treatment, including chemotherapy, radiation, and two stem-cell transplants. He's well now, and keeps his bear in his bedroom. "It's just unbelievable that a kid did this for another kid," said Andrew's mother, Margaret. A nine-year-old patient from Oklahoma also wrote to Crabtree after receiving one of her bears, which he named Little Scotty. "Any time I have a nightmare, I squeeze Little Scotty, and he gets rid of my bad dreams," the boy wrote. Needless to say, these stories are welcome confirmation to Crabtree that her years of hard work are making a difference in the lives of young people across North America.

—— " ——

A nine-year-old patient from Oklahoma wrote to Crabtree after receiving one of her bears, which he named Little Scotty. "Any time I have a nightmare, I squeeze Little Scotty, and he gets rid of my bad dreams," the boy wrote.

—— " ——

HONORS AND AWARDS

Entrepreneurial Achievement Award (Ernst & Young): 1999
George Washington Honor Medal (Freedom Foundation at Valley Forge): 1999
Honorary Membership (Young Entrepreneurs' Organization): 1999
Born Hero (Lands' End): 2000
Star Kid (*American Girl* magazine): 2001
Angels in Action Award (Angel Soft): 2004

FURTHER READING

Books

Giovagnoli, Melissa. *Angels in the Workplace*, 1999

Periodicals

Business Journal, Feb. 18, 2000, p.1
People, Jan. 16, 2006, p.97

Online Articles

http://www.signonsandiego.com/news/solutions/20041126-9999-1mc26
   bears.html
   (*San Diego Union Tribune,* "Bear Business Keeps Girl Busy, Helps Cancer
   Patients," Nov. 26, 2004)

ADDRESS

Taylor Crabtree
TayBear
993 South Santa Fe Avenue, #C339
Vista, CA 92083

WORLD WIDE WEB SITE

http://www.taybearhugs.org

Roger Federer 1981-

Swiss Professional Tennis Player
Four-Time Wimbledon Men's Champion and Winner
of Nine Grand Slam Titles

BIRTH

Roger Federer was born in Bern, Switzerland, on August 8,
1981. His mother, Lynette, is South African, and his father,
Robert, is Swiss. Federer's parents were both employed by the
Swiss pharmaceutical company Ciba-Geigy; they met when
his father was on a business trip to South Africa. Roger Federer has one older sister, Diana.

YOUTH

Federer was raised in Münchenstein, Switzerland, a German-speaking town. As a young child, he accompanied his parents to the tennis courts on weekends, but he spent most of the time running around with the other children while the adults played. By age four or so, however, he was playing himself, and when he was eight years old he joined a tennis club. He loved tennis from the start. "I always loved to play against the garage door or against the cupboard doors inside," he recalled. "My mum got fed up because it was bang, bang, bang all day."

—————— **"** ——————

Federer struggled during his early teens, when tennis took him away from his family for extended periods. But his mother says that "those struggles were good for him, a challenge. He learned to be independent, and to develop as a person."

—————— **"** ——————

Federer's development as a player was greatly aided by Peter Carter, an Australian coach who instructed the youngster from ages 10 to 14. Carter helped Federer develop his one-handed backhand and emphasized technique and professionalism, and by his early teens the youngster was one of the top junior players in all of Switzerland.

Federer's game received another boost when he reluctantly decided to leave soccer — another game he loved — behind to focus on tennis. "I prefer to be in control of what's happening, whereas in soccer if the goalie makes a mistake, everyone has to pay for it," he explained. "I also thought I was better at tennis, and I got results faster. I think in the end I probably enjoyed playing tennis more." Besides, as he pointed out on another occasion, "I was pretty good at soccer, but I was the Swiss national junior champ in tennis, so there was no way I could quit."

At age 13 Federer left home to be trained with other promising junior players at the Swiss national tennis center in the French-speaking town of Ecublens. He lived at the training center during the week and visited his family only on weekends. These periods of separation, combined with the challenges of learning a new language, left him extremely homesick during the first few months. His mother recalled that her son often cried on Sunday evenings when it was time for him to return to Ecublens. But she says that "those struggles were good for him, a challenge. He learned to be independent, and to develop as a person."

EDUCATION

Federer combined tennis instruction and school until age 16, when he decided to quit school to concentrate on his sports training. "I felt school was disturbing me of being 100 percent focused on tennis," he claimed. His parents understood his decision, but according to Federer, they also said "that if, in the next few years, you don't have any results, you go back to school."

Federer resumed training with Carter, who had moved on to a coaching position at the Swiss tennis training center in Biel. The promising young star quickly proved that his self-confidence had not been misplaced. "I finished as No. 1 junior in the summer and everything was going my way," he recalled.

CAREER HIGHLIGHTS

Federer made his professional debut in March 1998, playing doubles in the Greece F1 tournament with Martin Verkerk of the Netherlands. They were soundly beaten in the first round. Later that summer, though, the 16-year-old Federer won both the junior singles and junior doubles championships at Wimbledon. He was delighted with the victories, but skipped the gala winners' reception in London. Instead, he flew home to Switzerland to play in his first professional singles match at the Gstaad International Series tournament. He lost in straight sets, and had very limited success in other pro events that year. But in December Federer won the RADO Orange Bowl Tennis Championship, a junior-level hard-court event held in Key Biscayne, Florida. He thus finished his first year of professional play with only two wins and four losses—hardly a sensational debut. But the RADO championship also enabled him to end the year as the top-ranked junior men's player in the world.

In 1999 Federer left junior competition behind and began showing his talents on the professional stage. He advanced to the quarterfinals and semifinals of a number of smaller tournaments, showing flashes of tremendous ability. In November 1999 Federer even won his first professional title, claiming the Brest International Tournament Championship with a 7-6, 6-3 defeat of the Belorussian Max Mirnyi.

Tennis scoring can seem complicated. In men's tennis, players usually play best 3 out of 5 sets, though some tournaments use a best 2-out-of-3 format. The first player to win 6 games usually wins the set, but if their margin of victory is less than 2 games, the set is decided by a tiebreaker. Shorthand notation is often used to show the score of a tennis match. For example, 6-2, 6-3, 4-6, 7-6 means that the player in question won the first

Federer in action during the French Open in 1999.

set by a score of 6 games to 2, won the second set by a score of 6 games to 3, lost the third set by a score of 4 games to 6, and clinched the match by winning in a fourth-set tiebreaker. In a tiebreaker, the winner is the first player to score seven or more points, and lead by two.

Federer was less successful, however, in the tour's "Grand Slam" events. These are the four biggest annual events in professional tennis — the Australian Open, the French Open, the U.S. Open, and Wimbledon. To his great disappointment, he was knocked out of both the French Open and Wimbledon in the opening round of competition. Still, the 18-year-old Federer ended the year 1999 as the 64th ranked player in the world in men's play, according to the Association of Tennis Professionals (ATP).

High Expectations

Despite Federer's youth and modest early success in the professional ranks, many observers claimed that he had the potential to become a top-ranked player. This buzz actually proved to be a distraction. "Because people were constantly saying I was talented and that I was going to make it, I always had that burden," Federer recalled. "It was like, if I make it, then I'm only doing what's expected of me, and if I don't, then I'm a disaster because I missed on a great career or wasted my talent."

The pressure to meet expectations—both his own and those of tennis "experts"—sometimes resulted in temper tantrums and other losses of composure during Federer's first couple of years on the ATP tour. "I used to have a very bad temper on court," he admitted. "I was so disappointed with the way I played, even my opponents would comfort me." Over time, however, Federer learned to keep his emotions under control out on the court. "Today I'm much more in control of myself," he said in 2006, "whereas before it was a weak point of my tennis. People would say, 'If you can get to him mentally, you've got it.' And now it's become a strong point in my game."

Another step forward in Federer's professional growth took place in September 2000, when he represented his country in the Sydney Summer Olympic Games. He missed out on a medal, losing 7-6, 6-7, 6-3 in the bronze-medal match to Arnaud Di Pasquale of France. Still, Federer recalls the Sydney Olympics fondly. "It was one of the best experiences I've had as an athlete," he insisted. "There's nothing like the vibe in the Olympic Village, and I had a great time." Federer closed out the 2000 campaign with a 34-29 won-loss record and a ranking of 29th in the world.

> "Because people were constantly saying I was talented and that I was going to make it, I always had that burden," Federer recalled. "It was like, if I make it, then I'm only doing what's expected of me, and if I don't, then I'm a disaster because I missed on a great career or wasted my talent."

Toppling a Hero

Federer began the 2001 season with a bang, earning the Milan Indoor Championship in February with a victory over Julien Boutter of France (6-4, 6-7, 6-4). A few months later, he advanced all the way to the quarterfinals of the prestigious French Open before losing to Spain's Alex Corretja in straight sets (7-5, 6-4, 7-5).

But despite these promising results, no one was prepared for Federer's performance at the Wimbledon Championships a few weeks later. He rolled through his first three opponents, then defeated defending Wimbledon champion Pete Sampras in a hard-fought, five-set stunner (7-6, 5-7, 6-4, 6-7, 7-5). The shocking upset ended Sampras's 31-match winning streak at Wimbledon and served notice that the 19-year-old Federer was going to be a force to be reckoned with for years to come. "There are a lot of young guys coming up, but Roger is a bit extra-special," Sampras conceded. "He has a great all-around game."

Federer was knocked out of Wimbledon in the quarterfinals by Tim Henman of Great Britain, but he played consistently well for the next several months. He ended the year as the 13th ranked player in the world, with a record of 46 wins and 20 losses. Federer's roll continued in early 2002 as he claimed the championship of the Adidas International tournament in Sydney, Australia, and advanced to the fourth round of the Australian Open before losing a tough, five-set battle to Tommy Haas of Germany (7-6, 4-6, 3-6, 6-4, 8-6). At midseason, though, Federer went into a slump, exiting both the French Open and Wimbledon in the first round. It was at this moment that he was rocked by tragic news from Africa.

In the summer of 2002 Federer learned that Peter Carter, his mentor and former coach, had been killed in an automobile accident while on safari in South Africa. At first, it appeared that the news of Carter's death struck yet another blow to the young player's state of mind. In late August 2002 Federer appeared at the TD Waterhouse Cup tournament in Long Island, New York. He lost in his first match, falling to Chilean Nicolas Massu in a performance that Charles Bricker described in the *South Florida Sun-Sentinel* as "wild-swinging" and "confounding." "I've lost all confidence," Federer admitted afterward. "I feel like I'm missing energy."

Over the next several weeks, though, Federer came to grips with the death of his friend and coach. Some observers even believe that the tragedy forced him to grow up and to commit himself to tennis in a more disciplined manner. He regained his competitive spirit and put together a string of impressive finishes to close out the year, including the championship of the CA Tennis Trophy tournament in Vienna, Austria. By season's end he had a 55-22 record in match play, good enough to vault him to sixth place in the men's ranks.

Winning a Grand Slam

When the 2003 season began, many tennis experts believed that Federer was poised for a big year. He proved that their forecasts were on target, winning four tournaments in the season's opening weeks. Federer entered the prestigious Wimbledon Championships brimming with confidence, and he lost only one set in six matches to earn a spot in the men's singles final. Facing Australian Mark Philippoussis on tennis's biggest stage, Federer showed no signs of self-doubt or nervousness. Instead, he pounded Philippoussis in straight sets (7-6, 6-2, 7-6) in less than two hours. With this win Federer became the first Swiss man ever to win Wimbledon and

Federer returns a shot to Andre Agassi during the final of the Masters Cup, 2003.

the first to win a Grand Slam singles title. After the match was over, he broke down in tears and dedicated his historic victory to his former coach, Peter Carter. "I think of him every day," he said. "In these big matches, I thank him also inside. It gives me strength somehow."

Federer closed out the season in strong fashion, capping his terrific year with a straight set victory over Andre Agassi (6-3, 6-0, 6-4) in December to claim the Masters Cup Championship. *Sports Illustrated* writer L. Jon Wertheim expressed amazement at Federer's dominant win over Agassi, one of the game's legendary players: "Federer . . . showcased the manifold qualities required to succeed at tennis's highest level: athleticism, accuracy, cunning, power, and concentration. And, in his case, grace."

Federer ended the year ranked No. 2 in the world in men's tennis behind Andy Roddick. He also won $4 million in prize money in 2003 alone. But despite his growing fame and fortune, Federer refused to hire public relations agents or travel with a large entourage. "The more people you have around you, the less it becomes about the tennis," he explained. Federer did surprise the tennis world by firing his coach, Peter Lundgren, at the end of the 2003 season. "There was a benefit to figuring things out for myself and being more responsible for my preparation," he said. Since that time, Federer has played without a full-time coach.

World No. 1

After a holiday break, Federer was back on tour in early 2004. He won the first Grand Slam event of the year, the hard-court Australian Open in early February. In the final match he defeated Marat Safin of Russia (7-6, 6-4, 6-2). After the match, Safin told reporters that "I just lost to a magician." *Sports Illustrated* reached a similar conclusion after watching him in Australia, declaring that "[Federer] can execute every shot in the book — and a good many that aren't. He is equally adept at hitting with power and with touch; he is as cozy at the net as he is on the baseline."

Federer's victory in the Australian Open enabled him to slip past Andy Roddick as the top-ranked player in the ATP men's rankings. Over the next several weeks, he showed that he had no intention of giving up that spot. Federer successfully defended his title at the Dubai Tennis Open in March and won the Pacific Life Open in Indian Wells, California, two weeks later. He seemed nearly unstoppable as he rolled over opponents. He won on clay in Hamburg, Germany, and then on grass in the Gerry Weber Open in Halle, Germany (some tournaments, such as Wimbledon, are played on grass; others are played on clay and hardcourt).

> "
>
> *After Federer defeated Andy Roddick in the 2004 Wimbledon finals, Roddick joked that "I threw the kitchen sink at him, but he went to the bathroom and got his tub."*
>
> "

In June 2004 Federer returned to the All-England Lawn Tennis Club in Wimbledon to defend his title. He beat Lleyton Hewitt of Australia and Sebastian Grosjean of France on the way to a finals match-up with Roddick. Using his powerful serve, which has been clocked at more than 150 miles per hour, Roddick won the first set. Federer, though, came back to win the second. With Roddick leading the third set four games to two, rain interrupted play. After the delay, Federer abandoned his usual baseline game in favor of a serve and volley strategy. (Serve and volley is when a player serves and then quickly moves toward the net to hit the return ball before it bounces.) Using a variety of tactics, Federer eventually triumphed 4-6, 7-5, 7-6, 6-4 to claim his second straight Wimbledon title. Afterward, Roddick joked, "I threw the kitchen sink at him, but he went to the bathroom and got his tub."

Federer also won the final Grand Slam event of the year, the 2004 U.S. Open in Flushing Meadows, New York. Federer defeated Lleyton Hewitt,

Federer and Agassi shaking hands during the 2004 U.S. Open.

who had won 16 matches in a row coming into the championship, in straight sets (6-0, 7-6, 6-0) in the men's final. With this triumph, Federer became the first player since Sweden's Mats Wilander in 1988 to win three Grand Slam events in the same year. Federer finished the year with a total of 70 wins, 5 losses, and 11 singles championships.

Going for the Records

As the 2005 season got underway, the 23-year-old Federer stood as the undisputed number one player in the world. "There's no one who can play with him today," claimed Sampras. "For the next four or five years, his competition will be the record books." A semifinal loss to Safin at the Australian Open, however, put to rest any talk that Federer might make a sweep of the year's Grand Slam events. "It is really unfortunate," Federer said after the loss. "I thought I played really well and a point here and there changed the match. That was a pity, but at least I gave it a fight."

Putting this disappointment behind him, Federer went on to dominate the men's tour for much of the year. He won 11 titles, including two Grand Slam events: Wimbledon and the U.S. Open. His U.S. Open victory over Andre Agassi was particularly important to Federer. "This is the most special one for me, to play Andre in the final of the U.S. Open," he said. "He's one of the only living legends in tennis we still have." For his part, Agassi was very gracious in defeat, calling Federer "the best I've ever played against. . . . He plays the game in a very special way. I haven't seen it before."

Federer ended the 2005 season with a record of 80 wins and only four losses. In naming him the player of the year, *Tennis* magazine noted that Federer "put together a special season, one that will be nearly impossible for anyone to match in the near future — except, perhaps, Federer himself. . . . [It's] clear that fans are witnessing an unprecedented stretch of dominance in the men's game."

> *Federer admitted that his triumph over Rafael Nadal in the 2006 Wimbledon final "was important for me. . . . When we play so often in finals, it adds something to the game. He's up-and-coming. I used to be the youngster. Now I'm sort of getting older. But it's a great rivalry."*

The Emergence of a Rival

One of Federer's few defeats in 2005 had come in the French Open against nineteen-year-old Rafael Nadal of Spain, who eventually won the tournament. As the 2006 season began, it was clear that Federer wanted to earn a French Open title — the only one of the Grand Slam events that he had yet to win. But observers pointed out that of the 41 singles titles earned by Federer to that point, only five had been played on clay, the surface for the French Open. In addition, Nadal defeated Federer twice in the weeks leading up to the French Open. The stage was set for an exciting duel in Paris.

Federer and Nadal, who were ranked No. 1 and No. 2 in the world, cruised through the early rounds of the French Open to face each other in the final. The match was highly anticipated because if Federer won he would become the first player to simultaneously hold all Grand Slam titles since 1969. Federer quickly won the first set, but Nadal fought back to win his second French Open (1-6, 6-1, 6-4, 7-6). After the match, Nadal praised Federer, describing him as "the best player I ever played, the best in history, the most complete."

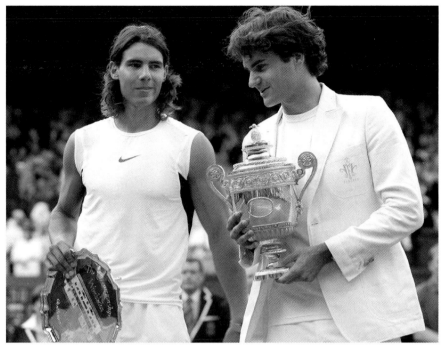

Wearing his custom sport coat, Federer holds the trophy after winning the men's final match against Rafael Nadal at Wimbledon, 2006.

One month later, on the grass courts at Wimbledon, Federer faced his rival once again in the men's final. But this time Federer prevailed, defeating Nadal in four hard-fought sets (6-0, 7-6, 6-7, 6-3) to win a record fourth-straight Wimbledon singles title. "It was important for me to win a final against him for a change," admitted Federer. "When we play so often in finals, it adds something to the game. He's up-and-coming. I used to be the youngster. Now I'm sort of getting older. But it's a great rivalry."

Among the Best of All Time

In September 2006 Federer beat Roddick to clinch his third-consecutive U.S. Open and ninth Grand Slam title — only five fewer than the all-time leader in Grand Slam victories, Pete Sampras. Many people now view Federer as perhaps the best player in the history of the game, with the same level of dominance over his sport that Michael Jordan enjoyed in basketball and Tiger Woods has in golf. As former Australian tennis great Rod Laver said, "he has all the ingredients. With the way he plays under pressure, he has every chance of real greatness."

Many of these same observers give special recognition to the graceful but powerful way that Federer plays tennis. "Federer is the sport's jazz virtuoso, a living legend admired by tennis classicists," wrote Stephen Tignor in *Tennis*. "He moves beautifully and wins comprehensively." Sportswriter Scott Athorne agreed, writing in the *Sunday Times* that "Federer is playing a brand of tennis that has never been seen before. He is combining the classic grace and artistry of yesteryear with the modern power game. . . . Technically, he is perfect."

In assessing his own legacy, though, Federer likes to dwell on the way he carries himself in the swirl of money and stardom that surrounds him on a daily basis. "I would like to be remembered as a fair player," he said. "Also being polite with the people, because in life you can count on the elevator going in both directions—you always meet people twice, once on the way up and once on the way down."

> "I would like to be remembered as a fair player," Federer said. "Also being polite with the people, because in life you can count on the elevator going in both directions—you always meet people twice, once on the way up and once on the way down."

HOME AND FAMILY

Federer lives in Oberwil, Switzerland, with Miroslava Vavrinec, a former tennis player whom he met while both were representing Switzerland in the 2000 Summer Olympics in Sydney, Australia. Given his tour schedule, promotional events, and other engagements, Federer spends most of the year traveling. He estimates that he only spends about 60 days a year at his home.

HOBBIES AND OTHER INTERESTS

Federer enjoys beach vacations, deep-sea fishing, ping-pong, playing cards, video games, and musical theater. During tournaments he communicates with his fans worldwide through an online diary on his official Web site (http://www.rogerfederer.com/en/). He owns the RF Cosmetics company, which produces aftershave, cologne, and other products for men. In 2003 Federer founded a charitable organization to benefit children in South Africa and to support sports for children throughout the world. Since April 2006 he has also served as a Goodwill Ambassador for UNICEF.

HONORS AND AWARDS

Wimbledon Junior Championship: 1998
ITF World Junior Champion: 1998
Wimbledon Championship: 2003, 2004, 2005, 2006
ATP Player of the Year: 2004, 2005
Australian Open Tennis Championship: 2004, 2006
ITF World Champion: 2004, 2005
Player of the Year (*Sports Illustrated*): 2004
U.S. Open Championship: 2004, 2005, 2006
ESPY Best Male Tennis Player: 2005, 2006
Laureus World Sports Awards: 2005, 2006, for sportsman of the year
Men's Player of the Year (*Tennis*): 2005
Player of the Year (*Tennis*): 2006

FURTHER READING

Periodicals

Atlantic Monthly, July-Aug. 2006, p.164
Current Biography International Yearbook, 2004
Interview, July 2006, p.64
New York Times, July 9, 2006; Aug. 20, 2006, p.47; Sep. 11, 2006, p.D1
South Florida Sun-Sentinel, Aug. 25, 2002, p.C16
Sports Illustrated, July 14, 2003; Dec. 29, 2003, p.106; Feb. 9, 2004, p.64; July 12, 2004, p.46; Oct. 4, 2004, p.78; Jan. 17, 2005, p.62; Sep. 19, 2005; June 19, 2006, p.56; July 17, 2006, p.56
Sports Illustrated for Kids, Sep. 1, 2005, p.56
Sunday Times (London), June 20, 2004, p.13; Mar. 5, 2006, p.48
Tennis, June 1999, p.16; Jan.-Feb.2006, p.34; June 2006, p. 44; July 2006, p.62
Time, Sep. 4, 2006, p. 60
Time Atlantic, Aug. 16, 2004, p.53
Time International, Jan. 24, 2005, p.36
Vogue, Dec. 2004, p.348

Online Articles

http://news.bbc.co.uk/sport2/hi/in_depth/2001/wimbledon_2001/1418928
    .stm
    (*BBC Sport*, "Federer Ends Sampras Reign," July 2, 2001)
http://news.bbc.co.uk/sport2/hi/tennis/4207905.stm
    (*BBC Sport*, "Safin Stuns Federer in Epic Semi," Jan. 27, 2005)

http://www.rolandgarros.com/en_FR/news/articles/2006-06-11/200606
111150039906600.html
  (*Roland Garros: The 2006 French Open Official Site,* "Nadal Faces Down
  Federer to Defend Crown," June 11, 2006)
http://www.tennis-x.com/fun/federerfile.php
  (*Extreme Tennis News,* "The Roger Federer File," Feb. 17, 2004)

Online Databases

Biography Resource Center Online, 2006, article from *Newsmakers,* 2004

Additional information for this profile came from an interview with Roger
  Federer for "The Charlie Rose Show" (conducted on September 13,
  2004).

ADDRESS

Roger Federer
Postfach
4103 Bottmingen
Switzerland

WORLD WIDE WEB SITES

http://www.atptennis.com
http://www.rogerfederer.com
http://www.tennis.com
http://www.usopen.org
http://www.wimbledon.org

June Foray 1917-
American Voice Actor
The Voice behind Rocket J. Squirrel on "The
Bullwinkle Show" and Hundreds of Other Popular
Animated Characters in Cartoons and Films

BIRTH

June Foray was born on September 18, 1917, in Springfield,
Massachusetts. Her mother was a semiprofessional pianist
and singer. Her father was an engineer.

YOUTH

Though she would eventually become an actress, acting was not Foray's first dream for a show business career. She first considered a career in dance, after seeing the fame and talent of Eleanor Powell, a tap dancing star who had grown up in Springfield. But Foray abandoned her plans after a prolonged bought of pneumonia. Her mother, a talented pianist, encouraged her to develop her musical talents. But Foray didn't share her mother's enthusiasm for music, and when she broke her finger playing basketball she happily gave up her piano lessons.

By age six, Foray announced that she would become an actress. She traced the beginning of her life as an actress to the Springfield Public Library. "I would memorize the classics, and walk around the neighborhood, pretending to be all those wonderful characters," she recalled. Her parents supported her dream, taking her to movies, the theater, and opera performances. She soaked up all that she saw and recalled that she would "impersonate everybody" when she returned home. Her love of acting led her to a part in "just about every school play that was put on," she said. "But I'm only 4 feet 11. I wanted to be on stage, but what are you going to do when you're this short? So I went into radio."

> As a teen, Foray's love of acting led her to a part in "just about every school play that was put on," she said. "But I'm only 4 feet 11. I wanted to be on stage, but what are you going to do when you're this short? So I went into radio."

Foray's life in radio began at age 12, when she appeared on a local radio program that was produced by her school drama teacher. Within three years she had joined the WBZA Players, a repertoire company in Springfield, and contributed regularly to local radio plays. When Foray was 17 her family moved to Los Angeles. Soon after her arrival, the ambitious young actress landed roles on Hollywood-produced national programs such as *The Jimmy Durante Show, The Danny Thomas Show,* and the *Lux Radio Theatre.*

Foray's talent attracted the attention of producers throughout the entertainment industry, and by the end of her teens she was appearing on two or three radio programs a day. At age 19 Foray was given her own children's radio program, *Lady Makebelieve.* This program, in which Foray read her own children's stories over the airwaves, was broadcast by the Los Angeles Board of Education into district classrooms for three years.

EDUCATION

Foray attended elementary school in the Springfield public school system, and she split her high school years between Massachusetts and California. Foray's acting career started before she finished high school. Sources suggest that she completed high school, but the date of her graduation is unknown.

CAREER HIGHLIGHTS

Starting work at such a young age, Foray developed most of her expertise on the job. "Radio was the greatest training ground," she said. "You had to be very quick and you had to be very versatile." Foray was both. Comedian and radio star Stan Freberg declared that Foray was "quite simply, the best in the business. I could write anything, confident in the knowledge that whatever the age, whatever the accent, June could do it."

During the 1940s Foray became known for her voice work on Jerry Fairbanks' *Speaking of Animals* short films, in which she was the voice of a filmed animal with an animated mouth. She also began recording children's records for Capitol Records with Stan Freberg, Daws Butler, and Mel Blanc.

Neither Foray nor Blanc knew it, but this collaboration came at a time when both actors were just beginning to emerge as the two leading providers of many of America's most beloved cartoon voices. Blanc became a dominant figure in animated films and television shows over the next several decades, providing the voices of such memorable characters as Bugs Bunny, Elmer Fudd, Foghorn Leghorn, and Daffy Duck. Foray, meanwhile, became the most famous female voice-over actor. Her status prompted some people to call her "the female Mel Blanc." But Chuck Jones, Foray's friend and employer and one of the giants of American animation, asserted that "June Foray is not the female Mel Blanc. Mel Blanc was the male June Foray."

Working for Disney

Foray's work with Capitol Records brought her to the attention of Disney Studios. In 1950 she left radio for animated film for the first time, providing the vocals for Lucifer the Cat in the Disney film *Cinderella*. Next she played the voice of Witch Hazel in the short animated film *Trick or Treat*. Foray's voice for Witch Hazel became the standard from which almost every subsequent witch voice has been patterned. "I did so many witches I should have a wart out of my nose," Foray said of her many variations on Witch

Foray has voiced characters in many different films, including Lucifer the cat in Cinderella, *1950 (top); Cindy Lou Who in* How the Grinch Stole Christmas, *1966 (center); and Granny in many animated adventures featuring Sylvester and Tweety Pie, including this shot from* The Looney, Looney, Looney Bugs Bunny Movie, *1981 (bottom).*

Hazel. She then created the voices for an Indian squaw and a mermaid in the 1953 animated feature *Peter Pan*.

That same year Foray unveiled one of her most famous and enduring voices: that of Granny, the owner of Tweety Pie the canary and Sylvester the cat. She first brought Granny to life in *A Streetcat Named Sylvester*, produced by Warner Brothers. Foray then continued to supply the voice of Granny in Sylvester and Tweety Pie cartoons for the next 15 years. She also provided Granny's voice in the late 1990s, when the WB Network broadcast a new cartoon series, "The Sylvester and Tweety Mysteries."

The Voice of Rocky

In 1958 Jay Ward, the creator of the first animated television series, "Crusader Rabbit," approached Foray with an interesting job offer. He asked Foray to provide the voice of Rocket J. Squirrel, a spunky squirrel in a pilot for an animated series called "Rocky and His Friends." Ward's idea was to create a type of animated variety show that would satirize contemporary American life. He especially wanted to comment on the "Cold War." The Cold War began at the end of World War II and finally came to an end with the collapse of the Soviet Union in 1991. The term Cold War refers to a period of political, military, and economic rivalry between the United States and the Soviet Union—and their respective allies. It was marked by deep distrust, continuing hostility, and sometimes open conflict among many nations in the world.

Foray happily signed up for the role of Rocky, which would become the most famous of her entire career. She recalls that when she asked Ward what sort of voice he would like for Rocky, he responded that he "just wanted Rocky to be a little, All-American boy." Foray responded by actually using her own voice for the little squirrel. Her decision proved to be a wise one.

The show, which starred Rocky the flying squirrel and his devoted, dimwitted friend Bullwinkle J. Moose, was an immediate hit. Children and parents alike loved watching the duo match wits with Mr. Big, an evil midget, and his spies from the fictional Pottsylvanian, Boris Badenov and Natasha Fatale. Another popular aspect of the show was its use of short animated segments. These included "Fractured Fairy Tales," which parodied traditional children's stories; "Adventures of Dudley Do-Right," which followed Canadian Mountie Dudley Do-Right's battles against the evil Snidely Whiplash; and "Peabody's Improbable History," which followed an intelligent talking dog and a young boy name Sherman as they traveled back in time to various historical eras.

ABC broadcast "Rocky and His Friends" from 1959 to 1961. During this time, Foray not only provided the voice of Rocky, but also of Natasha Fatale, Nell Fenwick — the innocent object of Canadian Mountie Dudley Do-Right's affections — and many other characters. The show then moved to NBC, where it became the first prime-time animated series in network television history. The show, which was renamed "The Bullwinkle Show" when it moved to NBC, ran until 1964.

———— **"** ————

"The children enjoyed [Rocky and Bullwinkle] because of the humorous look of the characters and the sounds of the voices," said Foray. "The adults find it so inventive because of the puns, the satire. . . . It was a show that was different from everything that came before it or after it."

———— **"** ————

A Show for Everyone

Rocky and Bullwinkle's enduring popularity stemmed from the ability of their creators to combine adult-friendly humorous commentary about the Cold War and other current events with goofy hijinks that appealed to young children. "The children enjoyed it because of the humorous look of the characters and the sounds of the voices," confirmed Foray. "The adults find it so inventive because of the puns, the satire. . . . It was a show that was different from everything that came before it or after it."

The writers wrote to amuse themselves, poking fun at everyone and everything. "We offended everybody, of course — presidents, congressmen, actors," remembered Foray. "We spared no one." Not surprisingly, many people in the animation business expressed great admiration for the show and its approach. As the legendary animator Chuck Jones said in the *New York Times,* "Bugs, Daffy Duck, Wile E. Coyote . . . were character actors, funny for what they did. Rocky and Bullwinkle were stand-up comics, funny for what they said." The clever humor convinced viewers to overlook the show's terrible soundtrack and budget-conscious animation. "Sometimes Boris had only half a mustache," Foray remembered.

Foray has many fond memories of those Rocky and Bullwinkle years. She recalls that for each show, the actors would assemble in Ward's studio, read the script once before recording, and tape it in one sitting. "The only time we ever did it over was when we'd go too long, or I'd laugh too much," Foray related. She also enjoyed the challenge of instantly switching voices between Rocky and Natasha when they were placed in scenes together.

Rocky J. Squirrel, Bullwinkle J. Moose, Natasha Fatale, and Boris Badenov from "Rocky and His Friends."

"Rocky would say, 'Hokey smoke, haven't I seen you before?' And then I'd say, 'No, dahling,' in the same breath," she said. "I had to have different colored pencils so I would know what part was coming up."

The task of delivering multiple voices was even greater for Foray in some of the "Fractured Fairy Tales" segments. In a few of these pieces, Foray would deliver lines from princesses, fairy godmothers, and witches, all one after another in quick succession. Years later, she recalled her work on those shows with great affection. "It was like working in a beautiful insane asylum," Foray remembered. "The scripts were brilliant satire and mordantly witty."

More than four decades after Rocky the squirrel made his debut, it is that voice that is most closely associated with Foray. In fact, she claims that complete strangers sometimes identify her as the voice of Rocky when she is out shopping. But her career continued long after the creators stopped making new Rocky and Bullwinkle adventures. She did voice work well into her eighties, playing hundreds of different animated characters. Her most recent high-profile job was as the voice of Grandmother Fa in the 1998 Disney film *Mulan.*

Inspired by Literature

Throughout her long and distinguished career, Foray has often claimed that her love of reading was an essential factor in her success. She says that literature provided the inspiration she needed to develop such believable characters. Foray based her "little old lady" voice, for instance, on her reading of James M. Barrie's *The Old Woman Shows Her Medals:* "I used to memorize all of her speeches, and all the speeches of Lady Bracknell in *Importance of Being Earnest.* That's what I do."

Foray has encouraged young actors to develop a similar appreciation for literature. "Read — read literature, read out loud, learn to develop characters." Foray never discounted the importance of knowing how to act, however. To be a good voice-over actor, she once said, "you have to be an actress first and a voice technician second. It's not just a matter of changing your voice. You have to become the creation, to assume the attitude. Otherwise it's just one-dimensional."

Foray has complained over the years that a lot of the animated children's television shows have become "simplistic and condescending." But she also appreciates some of the work done by men and women in the industry. To honor those individuals, Foray founded the Annie Awards in 1972 through her membership in the Association Internationale du Film d'Animation (ASIFA). Each year, the Annie Awards honor the top achievements in the art of animated films. In the 1990s, Foray's contributions to the world of animation inspired ASIFA-Hollywood, the organization's U.S. chapter, to create the June Foray Award to honor individuals who significantly and benevolently impact the art and industry of animation. She received the first June Foray Award in 1995. In 2000, in a testimony to her enduring popularity, Foray was honored with a star on the Hollywood Walk of Fame in Hollywood, California.

MARRIAGE AND FAMILY

Foray married the writer Hobart Donovan in 1954. The couple had no children. Donovan died in 1976.

SELECTED CREDITS

As Voice of Rocket J. Squirrel

"Rocky and His Friends," voice of Rocky and other characters, 1959-61
  (TV series)
"The Bullwinkle Show," voice of Rocky and other characters, 1961-62
  (TV series)

Of Moose and Men, 1991 (film)
The Adventures of Rocky & Bullwinkle, 2000 (film)

As Voice of Witch Hazel

Trick or Treat, 1952 (short film)
Broom-Stick Bunny, 1956 (short film)
A Witch's Tangled Hare, 1959 (short film)
A-Haunting We Will Go, 1966 (short film)
"The Bugs Bunny Show," 1960-68 (TV series)

As Voice of Granny

A Streetcat Named Sylvester, 1953 (short film)
This Is a Life? 1955 (short film)
Red Riding Hoodwinked, 1955 (short film)
A Pizza Tweety Pie, 1958 (short film)
A Bird in a Bonnet, 1958 (short film)
"The Bugs Bunny Show," 1960-68 (TV series)
The Looney, Looney, Looney Bugs Bunny Movie, 1981 (film)
"The Sylvester & Tweety Mysteries," 1995-2000 (TV series)
Space Jam, 1996 (film)
Tweety's High Flying Adventure, 2000 (film)

Other Character Voices

Cinderella, voice of Lucifer the cat, 1950 (film)
"The Flintstones," voice of Betty Rubble, 1964 (TV pilot)
Frosty the Snowman, multiple voices, 1969 (film)
"The Tom and Jerry Show," voice of Jerry, 1966-72 (TV series)
How the Grinch Stole Christmas! voice of Cindy Lou Who, 1966 (film)
The Phantom Tollbooth, multiple voices, 1970 (film)
Rikki-Tikki-Tavi, voice of Mother, 1975 (film)
"The Smurfs," voices of Jokey Smurf and Mother Nature, 1981-90
    (TV series)
"The Gummi Bears," voice of Grammi Gummi, 1985-89 (TV series)
Who Framed Roger Rabbit?, multiple voices, 1988 (film)
Mulan, voice of Grandmother Fa, 1998 (film)

HONORS AND AWARDS

June Foray Award (Association Internationale du Film d'Animation): 1995

FURTHER READING

Books

Scott, Keith. *The Moose that Roared: The Story of Jay Ward, Bill Scott, a Flying Squirrel and a Talking Moose,* 2000

Periodicals

Advertising Age, Dec. 1, 1986, p.57
Back Stage West, July 20, 2000, p.25
Los Angeles Daily News, June 29, 2000, pp.L3, L6
Los Angeles Times, May 3, 1985, p.1; Nov. 13, 1988, p.6; June 20, 1994, p.F6; June 29, 2000, p.F22
People, May 20, 1991, p.75
Seattle Times, June 29, 2000, p.D4

Online Articles

http://www.awn.com/mag/issue5.03/5.03pages/evanierforay.php3
    (*Animation World Magazine,* "The Remarkable June Foray," June 2000)
http://starbulletin.com/96/07/11/features/story3.html
    (*Honolulu Star-Bulletin,* "Women Find Place in Humor's Boys' Club," July 11, 1996)
http://movies2.nytimes.com/gst/movies/filmography.html?p_id=24175
    (*New York Times,* "June Foray," undated)

ADDRESS

June Foray
Don Pitts Voices
11365 Ventura Blvd., Suite 100
Studio City, CA 91604

WORLD WIDE WEB SITE

http://www.annieawards.com/juneforayaward.htm

Alicia Keys 1981-
American Singer, Composer, and Pianist
Winner of Nine Grammy Awards

BIRTH

Alicia Keys was born on January 25, 1981 in Manhattan, New York. Her birth name was Alicia Augello Cook. Her mother, Terri Augello, a paralegal and part-time actress, is white. Her father, Craig Cook, a flight attendant, is black. Her father, though, was not around for most of her childhood. "He didn't live with me, he didn't raise me, I don't call him Dad," she said. Keys has a younger half-brother, Cole, on her father's side, but they did not grow up together.

Keys has said that she loves both sides of her heritage. "I grew up in New York, and thank God, I never had to go through that in regards to 'you're not black enough, you're not white enough, the whole kind of white/black mixture thing,'" she said. "I never had to go through that. I went through prejudices and all, surely. But I never had to battle with those two parts of me. . . New York is so diverse and there are so many different types of people. People couldn't care less what you are."

YOUTH

Keys grew up with her mother in a small, one-bedroom apartment in "Hell's Kitchen," a tough Manhattan neighborhood that had long been riddled by crime and poverty. (In recent years, this area has seen many improvements.) Her mother struggled to support herself and her daughter, often working two or three jobs a day. "My mom is definitely my rock," Keys said. "Growing up, we didn't have anybody but each other to survive in the city. She really helped me to become the person I am; the strong-mindedness that I have is all because of her."

> "My mom is definitely my rock," Keys said. "Growing up, we didn't have anybody but each other to survive in the city. She really helped me to become the person I am; the strong-mindedness that I have is all because of her."

Keys also credits her mother for inspiring her love of music. She remembers waking up on Sunday mornings to the sounds of her mother's jazz recordings, especially the music of Ella Fitzgerald, Billie Holiday, and Thelonious Monk. "I've had a deep love for music since I was four," Keys recalled. "Music came before everything, everything, everything." Keys discovered her singing talent in kindergarten, when her teacher chose her to play the starring role of Dorothy in a class production of the *Wizard of Oz*. "I shocked myself because I didn't realize I could sing," Keys said. "I was terrified to get on the stage. When I did, I felt free! Ms. Hazel [the teacher] is still around. I speak to her."

Keys began playing the piano when she was 7 years old. "A friend was getting rid of this old, brown upright piano she rarely played, and she agreed to let us have it if we'd move it from her apartment," Keys said. "We used the piano as a divider between our living room and my bedroom. That gift is one of the main reasons I'm playing today." Keys took piano lessons for the next several years, learning classical pieces by composers such as

Mozart, Beethoven, and Chopin. She practiced up to six hours a day. "I'm not going to sit here and lie and tell you I was happy practicing the scales every day when my friends were outside playing," she said, "My mom just wasn't having it, though. She was serious about my practicing first, then playing. And now, of course, I appreciate that."

Keys wrote her first song, "I'm All Alone," when she was 11. She wrote it after seeing the movie *Philadelphia,* which starred Denzel Washington as a lawyer who defends another lawyer, played by Tom Hanks, who is fired from his job after contracting AIDS. "I had just lost my grandfather and that movie made me reflect on what it was to lose somebody," Keys remembered. "I went home and sat down at the piano — it was so natural. I hadn't really allowed myself to feel that he had passed. I felt better to express that sadness." Keys never recorded the song in a studio, but she admits that a home recording of that song — and many others she wrote as a young girl — are stored in her New York apartment. "Some of it is very embarrassing," she admits with a laugh.

As Keys grew older, she became aware that the expense of her piano and dance lessons stretched her mother's already tight budget. She recalls that she repeatedly offered to quit. "But my mom would tell me, 'Quit what you like, but you're not quitting piano.' She didn't care what it cost," Keys said. Meanwhile, she received fascinating glimpses into the world of show business on days when her mother, unable to find a babysitter, brought her to theatre rehearsals. Watching all the actors work on a play was fascinating to Keys. "I'd take in how they'd transformed from when they first came in to when it was actually showtime," she said. "It was very inspiring. I was able to see the dream side — anything's possible. But I was also able to see the broken-dream side, the people who would never make it, and the way they had to survive as hookers on the streets of my neighborhood."

Keys has admitted that such grim surroundings made growing up more challenging for her. "Sure, there were times when I could have ended up in trouble," she said. "It's easy at that age to get caught up with people who are not necessarily doing the right thing and there were those people all around, but I had just enough sense to realize when things were getting over the top. I'm also lucky because my mother is such a strong woman, and she raised me to be strong and independent."

EDUCATION

When Keys was 12, she was accepted into the Professional Performing Arts School, a junior/senior public high school in New York City that was the setting for the 1980 movie *Fame* and subsequent television series. The students at this unique school go to academic classes in the mornings and then receive performing arts instruction at professional studios in the afternoons. Famous alumni of the school include the singer Britney Spears and the actress Claire Danes.

Keys developed a special bond with her music teacher, Linda Miller, during her years at the school. "She was eccentric, with beads and wooden bangles," Keys recalled. "We learned classical [music]. But she also wrote R&B [Rhythm and Blues] songs which she co-ordinated into the curriculum. She was the person who made me fall in love with harmonies. I surely loved them before then, but she fine-tuned my ear."

——— *"* ———

Music industry manager Jeff Robinson first saw Keys perform when she was 15. "I could see right away that she had a lot of soul as a singer, but there are lots of singers with that street twang," he recalled. "What really convinced me was when she sat down at a beat-up piano and began singing her own songs. I couldn't believe someone that young could be so fully developed musically."

——— *"* ———

An excellent student, Keys graduated from high school as her class valedictorian in 1995, when she was only 16. She then accepted a scholarship to attend Columbia University in New York City. It was around this same time that she changed her last name from Cook to Keys. The inspiration for the new name came from "lots of places," she explained. "Keys to opening doors, doors that have never been opened before. Keys to opportunity. Keys to life. And keys to the piano." She attended classes at Columbia briefly before leaving to devote all her energies to her singing career.

CAREER HIGHLIGHTS

Around age 14, Keys began a transition from playing classical piano to jazz and rhythm and blues. Around this same time, she began frequenting jazz clubs in Harlem, a primarily African-American neighborhood in Manhattan with a rich musical history. She also joined the girl's choir at the Police Athletic League Community Center in Harlem, practicing after school with vocal coach Conrad Robinson. Keys and a couple of other girls formed a group called EmBishion. Their repertoire included two songs written by Keys, "The Life" and "Butterflyz." Versions of both of these songs were later included on her first album, *Songs in A Minor*.

Keys performing in 2001.

Conrad Robinson told his brother, Jeff, a music-industry manager, about the talented young performer. Jeff Robinson first heard Keys sing at the community center when she was 15 years old. "I could see right away that she had a lot of soul as a singer, but there are lots of singers with that street twang," Jeff Robinson recalled. "What really convinced me was when she sat down at a beat-up piano and began singing her own songs. I couldn't believe someone that young could be so fully developed musically. She was the complete package. That's not something you see a lot these days."

Jeff Robinson encouraged Keys to pursue a career as a solo artist. Soon afterward, he signed her on as a client. He began booking her at music-industry shows, where influential people could hear her accompany herself on the piano. This period of travel and performing was made even more challenging by the heavy school load Keys was carrying. But Keys juggled her busy schedule without stumbling on stage or in the classroom.

One showcase performance, delivered without backup singers or an accompanying band for music-label executives, proved especially important to the young singer. The assembled executives were dazzled by her voice and piano playing. A bidding war ensued as industry executives competed to sign Keys to a recording contract. She ultimately decided to sign with Columbia Records, in part because the label included a baby grand piano for Keys in the contract.

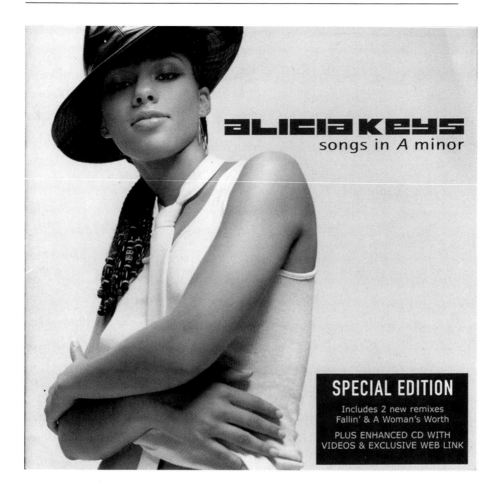

alicia keys
songs in *A* minor

SPECIAL EDITION
Includes 2 new remixes
Fallin' & A Woman's Worth
PLUS ENHANCED CD WITH
VIDEOS & EXCLUSIVE WEB LINK

Keys was ecstatic about her good fortune. But she soon discovered that juggling her recording career with the workload from her first semester at Columbia University was a daunting task. "I was always good at school . . . but Columbia is a whole other ball game!" she recalled. "I was coming in from the studio at four in the morning and getting up at eight to try and do my homework on the train to my classes—no way! I was the worst student ever at that point in my life, and I was so stressed." As a result, Keys dropped out of college four weeks into the first semester.

Keys hoped that this decision would help her music career, but as the weeks passed she repeatedly clashed with her music producers over her singing style and song selection. They also wanted to mold her image in a way that made Keys uncomfortable. "I felt that they wanted me to be a clone of Mariah [Carey] or Whitney [Houston] and I couldn't do that," she said. "I'm not the sequined dress type, or the high-heeled type, or the all-cleavage type," Keys said.

Robinson tried to intercede on her behalf, but the Columbia producers were determined to do things their way. The stalemate ended in 1998, when Keys performed for Clive Davis, the famous head of Arista Records. Davis had been instrumental in advancing the careers of such artists as Bruce Springsteen and Whitney Houston. He was bowled over by the young singer's talent and her beauty. Afterwards, he made a point of contacting Keys. "Clive was the only executive that ever asked me, how do I see myself, how do I see my career," she said. "When he asked me that question, I knew immediately that's where I had to be . . . What he sees for me, I see for myself." Davis quickly bought out her contract with Columbia and signed her with Arista.

Songs in A Minor

At Arista, Keys was finally able to record her album the way she wanted. She sat with producers and studio engineers to learn the process of recording music. "I knew the only way it would sound like anything I would be remotely proud of is if I did it," she said. "I already knew my way around a keyboard, so that was an advantage."

Meanwhile, the 17-year-old Keys left her mother's apartment and got her own place in Harlem. Soon after moving in, she installed a recording studio so that she could easily work on her music whenever the spirit moved her. "[Moving out] was necessary for my sanity," she said. "I was confused and all over the place. And I remember going to my mother's house, because that was where my only real piano was, and I wrote a song that was really a conversation with God. . . . I came back to Harlem and started to work on it, starting with the piano and building up with all the little things I was learning, and it became 'Troubles.' That's when the album started coming together. Finally, I knew how to structure my feelings into something that made sense, something that can translate to people. My confidence was up, way up." Soon afterward she wrote "Fallin,'" a soulful love ballad that later became a breakout hit.

Keys was very happy with how her debut album, which she had decided to call Songs in A Minor, was coming along. But just as it was nearing completion, Davis was forced out of Arista in an ugly battle for control of the label. The legendary executive subsequently formed his own label, J Records, and Keys signed on as one of the label's first artists. She admits that the delay in the release of her album due to the label switch "built my character and tested my confidence." But the wait proved to be worth it. In June

2001, *Songs in A Minor* was released on the J Records label. To the young singer's amazement, the 16-song album (including 14 songs written or co-written by Keys) debuted at number one on the charts.

Sudden Stardom

Most reviewers were quite impressed with Keys's combination of R&B, jazz, hip-hop and gospel music. In a review for the *Los Angeles Times*, Robert Hilburn called Keys "a singer-songwriter-pianist of immense potential." Hilburn added: "The reason for all the excitement is the 20-year-old New Yorker's remarkable range. She moves convincingly in the album from the Janet Jackson school of youthful Top 40 attitude in 'Girlfriend' to the funky sensuality of Prince's 'How Come U Don't Call Me Anymore' to the neo-soul vitality of Macy Gray and Jill Scott in Fallin.'"

———— **"** ————

"I thought I did good work and I hoped people would like [Songs in A Minor], but it's been crazy, the attention I've been getting," Keys said. "I'm like, 'Are you sure they want me on Leno?' or 'You're sure Prince wants to meet me?' It's bonkers."

———— **"** ————

Keys gave an additional boost to the album with various television appearances. She shot a popular music video for "Fallin'" that portrayed her as a broken-hearted young woman visiting her boyfriend in prison. At around the same time that the video aired on MTV, Davis arranged television appearances for Keys on "The Oprah Winfrey Show" and "The Tonight Show." This publicity further boosted record sales, and within a year of its release, six million copies of *Songs in A Minor* had been sold. The sudden fame and fortune was initially overwhelming for Keys. "It took off and it just didn't stop," she said. "I thought I did good work and I hoped people would like it, but it's been crazy, the attention I've been getting. I'm like, 'Are you sure they want me on Leno?' or 'You're sure Prince wants to meet me?' It's bonkers."

Keys also launched her first national tour in 2001, performing to enthusiastic audiences across the United States. She also appeared on a televised benefit concert for the families of the victims of the September 11, 2001, terror attacks, singing a moving rendition of Donny Hathaway's song "Someday We'll All Be Free." In January 2002 Keys won an American Music Award for favorite new artist in both the pop/rock and rhythm and blues categories. The following month, she captured five of the six

the diary of alicia keys

Grammy Awards for which she had been nominated, including song of the year for "Fallin,'" best new artist, and best R&B album for *Songs in A Minor*. She seemed stunned by all the accolades she received. "You don't know how much this humbles me," she said in one of her acceptance speeches.

The Diary of Alicia Keys

After the Grammy Awards, Keys resumed a busy touring schedule in the United States and Europe. Between concerts, she often wrote songs on a keyboard on her private tour bus or in her hotel room. Many of the songs appeared on her second album, *The Diary of Alicia Keys*, which was released in December 2003. The album sold more than 600,000 copies in its first week to vault to the top of the music charts.

Several guest artists accompany Keys on the album, including Kanye West, Harold Lilly, and Tim Mosley. A top-ten single from the *Diary*, "You Don't Know My Name," was called "gorgeous," and the "album's centerpiece," by Steve Jones in a four-star review of the album in *USA Today*. Keys's rendition of the song is "vulnerable yet in control as she makes a move on the object of her infatuation," Jones added. "It's a position she's often in as she covers a broad range of emotions." Other popular songs on the album include "Karma," "Heartburn," Dragon Days," and "Samsonite Man."

Keys's second album was also a big hit with critics and her fellow musicians. At the 2005 Grammy Awards, *The Diary of Alicia Keys* won three Grammies: best R&B album; best R&B song for "You Don't Know My Name" with Harold Lilly and Kanye West; and best female R&B vocal performance for "If I Ain't Got You." Keys also won a Grammy for "My Boo," a duet she recorded with Usher in 2004.

> ——— " ———
>
> *Keys enjoyed her spring 2004 "First Ladies Tour" with Beyoncé Knowles and Missy Elliott. "I think we all really respect each other and we really respect the work that each one does and we really have an admiration for each other," she said.*
>
> ——— " ———

The release of *The Diary of Alicia Keys* also took the young star back on tour. In March and April of 2004, Keys teamed up with the singers Beyoncé Knowles and Missy Elliott for what they called the "First Ladies Tour." The three Grammy-winning artists sang to sold-out crowds in 26 U.S. cities, making it one of the most successful tours of the year. According to Keys, there was no competition between the three stars. "I think we all really respect each other and we really respect the work that each one does and we really have an admiration for each other," she said.

In 2005 Keys unveiled *Alicia Keys Unplugged*, her first live album. The album, which was recorded before an audience at the Brooklyn Academy of Music in New York, included many of her biggest hits, including "Fallin'" and "You Don't Know My Name." Other highlights included "Intro A Capella," a prayer-like ballad that Keys sings without accompaniment; covers of the Prince songs "Heartburn" and "How Come You Don't Know Me"; as well as a gospel-inspired version of "Every Little Bit Hurts." Guest artists include the hip-hop artists Mos Def and Common, reggae star Damian Marley, and Maroon 5 singer Adam Levine. In a review for the *Boston Globe*, Renee Graham wrote that *Unplugged* proves

Keys performing at the 2005 Grammy Awards.

why "the singer-songwriter-pianist is one of the greatest talents of her generation."

Unplugged brought Keys yet another wave of Grammy Awards in 2006. She received a total of five nominations, including best R&B album for *Unplugged*, and best R&B song for "Unbreakable." For the first time in her career, though, she did not win any of the awards for which she was nominated.

Branching Out

Keys has kept a journal for years in which she has recorded her thoughts and feelings about her life and the world around her. Her journal also includes poetry, and in 2005 she combined several of these poems with lyrics to some of her songs in a book called *Tears for Water.* Many fans of her music embraced the book. But *Tears for Water* was not as well received by critics. Several reviewers commented that without her vibrant voice and accompanying music, the poems were of average quality. "These poems read like what they are — journal entries from a young woman — and they don't have great insight or clever wordplay," Jamie Watson wrote in *School*

Library Journal. "Even her song lyrics, so powerful when accompanied with lush piano arrangements, come across as banal when unadorned with instrumentation. However, both their creator and their subject matter will give these simple selections immense appeal with a teen audience. The writer talks about insecurities, personal growth, loneliness, and love — good, bad, long distance, and unrequited."

Writing a poetry book is just one of the ways that Keys has been diversifying her career. She has also begun a career as a film actress. "I grew up around the theater, my mother was an actress," she explained. "It's always been my destiny." She plays a major role, as an assassin, in the action-comedy *Smokin' Aces* (scheduled for release in 2007). Keys is excited about the film, which features an all-star cast that includes Ben Affleck, Don Cheadle, Jeremy Piven, and Andy Garcia. But she has also expressed some concern about how her part in the film will be received. "I think I have to put out a public service announcement for all my fans who are under 18," Keys said. "This role is that crazy. I get to deal with emotions that most people have to suppress, like extreme anger and rage."

> **Keys has expressed great excitement about branching out into acting. "I grew up around the theater, my mother was an actress," she explained. "It's always been my destiny."**

Keys has also signed on to star in *Composition in Black in White*, a film about the pianist and composer Philippa Schuyler. She was hand-picked to play Schuyler by the actress Halle Berry, who is producing the movie. Like Keys, Schulyer was a musical prodigy and the daughter of a mixed-race couple. Born 50 years earlier than Keys, in 1931, Schuyler struggled against racial and gender prejudice throughout her career.

HOME AND FAMILY

Alicia Keys lives in New York City, although she travels widely for her career and charity work. A very private person, Keys refuses to answer questions about her personal life. She acknowledges, though, that one of the first things she did after becoming successful was to buy her mother her own apartment in New York City. "That was really exciting to be able to decorate it," she recalled. "And she brought the oldest stereo. Before I was born she had this stereo. I said, 'What is this doing here? Get a new stereo!'"

HOBBIES AND OTHER INTERESTS

Keys likes to swim, read, and listen to music in her spare time. Her favorite musicians include Nina Simone, Duke Ellington, Miles Davis, Prince, Curtis Mayfield, Stevie Wonder, Carole King, Scott Joplin, and Marvin Gaye. "I like the old stuff," she remarked. She also likes coloring books. "I love those complex geometric books where I can sit on planes and just . . . color!" she said.

Keys has become active in charity work to benefit children. She supports Keep a Child Alive, an organization that provides medicine for children with AIDS. Her work with this organization led her to contribute the centerpiece essay to *How Can I Keep from Singing: Transforming the Lives of African Children and Families Affected by AIDS,* a 2006 photographic book that also features contributions from former U.S. President Bill Clinton and First Lady of South Africa Graça Machel.

She also is involved with a group called "Frum Tha Ground Up," which works to give teenagers the skills and opportunities to be successful. "Everything I do stems from something personal, not just because it will look good on paper or be a tax write-off," Keys said. "Camps are great, and I want to do one, but I want to be involved, hands-on. These possibilities give my life meaning, and they give me something other than the red carpet to look forward to."

SELECTED WORKS

Recordings

Songs in A Minor, 2001
The Diary of Alicia Keys, 2003
Alicia Keys Unplugged, 2005

Writings

Tears for Water: Songbook of Poems & Lyrics, 2004
How Can I Keep from Singing: Transforming the Lives of African Children and Families Affected by AIDS, 2006

SELECTED HONORS AND AWARDS

MTV Video Music Awards: 2001, Best New Artist in a Video, for "Fallin'"; 2004, Best R&B Video, for "If I Ain't Got You"; 2005, Best R&B Video, for "Karma"

Grammy Awards (National Academy of Recording Arts and Sciences): 2002, Song of the Year, for " Fallin'"; Best New Artist; Best Female R&B Vocal Performance, for "Fallin'"; Best R&B song, for "Fallin'"; Best R&B Album, for *Songs in A Minor*; 2005, Best R&B Song, for "You Don't Know My Name"; Best R&B Album, for *The Diary of Alicia Keys*; Best Female R&B Vocal Performance, for "If I Ain't Got You", Best R&B Performance by a Duo or Group with Vocals, for "My Boo" (with Usher)

American Music Awards: 2002, Favorite New Artist — Pop or Rock n' Roll; Favorite New Artist — Soul/Rhythm and Blues; 2004, Favorite Artist — Soul/Rhythm and Blues

NAACP Image Awards (National Association for the Advancement of Colored People): 2002, Outstanding New Artist; Outstanding Female Artist; 2004, Outstanding Female Artist; 2005, Outstanding Music Video, for "If I Ain't Got You"; Outstanding Song, for "If I Ain't Got You"; 2006, Outstanding Female Artist; Outstanding Song, for "Unbreakable"; Outstanding Music Video, for "Unbreakable"

Songwriter of the Year Award (American Society of Composers, Authors and Publishers): 2005, for rhythm and blues

FURTHER READING

Books

Bankston, John. *Alicia Keys,* 2004 (juvenile)
Current Biography, 2001
Horn, Geoffrey. *Alicia Keys,* 2005 (juvenile)
Keys, Alicia. *Tears for Water: Songbook of Poems & Lyrics*, 2004
Keys, Alicia. *How Can I Keep from Singing: Transforming the Lives of African Children and Families Affected by AIDS,* 2006
Who's Who in America, 2006

Periodicals

Daily Telegraph (London), Aug. 2, 2001, p.20; Oct. 8, 2005, Arts , p.4
Ebony, Jan. 2004, p.134
Los Angeles Times, June 24, 2001, p. 62
New York Times, Jan. 27, 2002, Arts and Leisure, p.1
O, The Oprah Magazine, Sept. 2004, p.256
Observer (London), Mar. 21, 2004, Music Magazine, p.32
Orlando Sentinel, Feb. 15, 2002, Visitor Guide, p.1
People, Oct. 17, 2005, p.93
Rolling Stone, Nov. 8, 2001, p. 82; Feb. 24, 2005, p.28
USA Today, Dec. 1, 2003, p.D5

Online Databases

Biography Resource Center Online, 2006, articles from *Contemporary Black Biography,* 2002, and *Notable Black American Women,* 2002

ADDRESS

Alicia Keys
c/o J Records
745 Fifth Avenue
New York, NY 10151

WORLD WIDE WEB SITE

http://www.aliciakeys.net

Cheyenne Kimball 1990-

American Singer and Songwriter
Star of the MTV Reality Series "Cheyenne"

BIRTH

Cheyenne Nichole Kimball was born on July 27, 1990, in
Jacksonville, North Carolina. She grew up in Frisco, Texas,
with her older sister Brittany. Her father, Brett, is a personal
fitness trainer who has worked with celebrities including the
singer Avril Lavigne and members of the bands Sum 41 and
Velvet Revolver. Cheyenne's mother, Shannon, has worked as
a personal trainer and advertising executive, but now serves as
Cheyenne's road manager.

YOUTH

Cheyenne has loved music for as long as she can remember. Her favorite childhood band was Blind Melon. "I remember very clearly the first time I heard [the song] "No Rain," she recalled on her website, www.cheyenne music.com. "It came on the radio—it had to be a few years after the record was out—and I was hooked. I just had to learn how to make those sounds." She was helped in that regard by a friend who gave her a guitar when she was seven years old. She quickly taught herself to play left-handed, and at age eight she wrote her first song, "All I Want is You." Cheyenne composed the song after being sent to her room for making a mean remark to her sister. "I remember writing it and hoping it would get me out of trouble," she admitted. "I haven't stopped writing songs or getting into trouble since."

Once she could play the guitar, Cheyenne kept asking her parents for permission to sing on street corners because she had heard that the Dixie Chicks started their career that way. Her parents always refused, but she remained undaunted. When nine-year-old Cheyenne entered herself in a talent night at a local club, her parents relented and let her perform. "I told my husband that because Cheyenne had never sung in a microphone or been in front of a crowd, we should let her do it and get it out of her system," Shannon Kimball recalled. To her parents' great surprise, though, Cheyenne sang with gusto and poise. "I turned and looked at my husband and we both knew she was born for this," said Cheyenne's mother. Cheyenne won second place in the contest.

> Cheyenne wrote her first song, "All I Want is You," after being sent to her room for making a mean remark to her sister. "I remember writing it and hoping it would get me out of trouble," she admitted. "I haven't stopped writing songs or getting into trouble since."

After the contest, Cheyenne began singing at clubs and coffee shops throughout Texas, accompanied by her mother. At age 12, armed with nearly 200 songs she had written herself, Cheyenne learned that auditions for the television show "America's Most Talented Kid" were being held in Dallas, Texas. Cheyenne's audition was successful, and she was booked on the series, which ran in 2003.

"America's Most Talented Kid," which originally aired on NBC, was hosted by the actor Mario Lopez. Children appearing on the show displayed different skills and talents, including singing, dancing, and magic tricks. There were three age groups in the competition: four to seven years old; eight to 12 years old; and 13 to 15 years old. Each performer was judged by the pop singer Lance Bass and two other guest judges. A winner was eventually decided in each age category and then an overall winner was crowned.

When Cheyenne's moment in the spotlight arrived, she selected the Sheryl Crow song "A Change Will Do You Good." Her strong singing and guitar playing vaulted her to first place in her age category (8 to 12 years). As the contest continued she performed some of her own songs, impressing the judges with every performance. In the season finale, the judges crowned her the overall "Most Talented Kid" winner, which came with a $50,000 prize. "I always really wanted to be a performer and the show really just kind of made it a reality, which was great," she remarked. "I figured I wouldn't get started until I was 16, but I got a little bit of a head start."

> "I don't really know what it [high school] is supposed to be like," Cheyenne said. "I feel like everything is balanced out. Even though I am going to miss out on my prom or I am going to miss out on walking across the stage to accept my diploma, that's okay to me because I know I will have other perks in life."

EDUCATION

Cheyenne was wrapping up middle school around the same time as her "Most Talented Kid" triumph. But her new-found fame got in the way of her studies. "She was hounded by students at her school to the point where she went from being a straight 'A' student, head cheerleader and class mediator to someone who didn't want to go," her mother explained. "We wound up home schooling which, as it turns out, was a good move."

Shannon Kimball served as Cheyenne's tutor until she began filming her television show *Cheyenne*. At that point executives at MTV hired a professional tutor for her. As a result, Cheyenne has never attended high school. "I don't really know what it [high school] is supposed to be like," she said. "I've seen movies and stuff. Even that is different than what normal high school is. I feel like everything is balanced out. Even though I am going to miss out on my prom or I am going to miss out on walking across the stage to accept my diploma, that's okay to me because I know I will have other perks in life."

CAREER HIGHLIGHTS

During the "America's Most Talented Kid" competition, Cheyenne appeared on NBC's "The Today Show," a morning television show. "Sony's head of global A & R, David Massey, saw me on the 'Today' show giving an interview before I had even won," she recalled. "He had no idea I was a musician. He was on the treadmill, watching TV on mute and he just saw how poised I was for 12 and was like, 'I need to find that girl!'"

Soon afterward, when Cheyenne was 13, she signed a multi-record deal with Sony/Epic Records and began working on her first album.. Although she had already written hundreds of songs, Cheyenne wanted new material. She collaborated on some songs with several veteran songwriters, including Billy Mann (who has worked with Joss Stone and Teddy Geiger) and Kara DioGuardi (who has worked with Ashlee Simpson and Lindsay Lohan). "I started completely fresh," she said. "My lyrics are not age based. If anything, I write a lot older than my age. Maybe I could outgrow them when I'm more mature, but they are always going to be the songs that introduced me to the world."

The Day Has Come

Cheyenne spent the next three years working on her debut album while still maintaining a challenging touring schedule. This period included six months in a California recording studio with bassist Brad Smith and guitarist Christopher Thorn, former members of Blind Melon, Cheyenne's favorite band. "When I was working on [the song] 'Everything to Lose' with the guys, I started to feel more confident than I ever had," she recalled on her website. "I can never thank them enough for helping me open up as a songwriter and teaching me how to let the music flow organically. I cried the day I left their studio because it felt like I was leaving home."

Cheyenne recorded more than 50 songs for the album, which she decided to call *The Day Has Come*. But there was only room for 12 songs on the album. The songs the young singer selected were more mature than her mother had expected. "People always think that I write Cheyenne's songs because they don't know how a girl that young could write about love," she said. She even joked that she occasionally looked under Cheyenne's bed to try and find the 30-year-old who was providing song lyrics to her daughter.

The signature piece of *The Day Has Come* was "Hanging On," which later became a hit single (and the theme song of her MTV series, *Cheyenne*). "It's a song about following your dreams and never letting things stand in your

way; basically what I've been doing all my life," Cheyenne explained. "The song was really important to me because it kept reminding me to be patient, which is something that I'm not very good at." The song "Four Walls" also has special significance to Cheyenne because she recorded it while her father was hospitalized with a severe infection. "What you hear of that song is not a performance," she said. "The emotion is coming from a very real and honest place."

"Cheyenne," the Television Series

About midway through the recording of *The Day Has Come,* Cheyenne and her parents were approached by MTV executives about doing a television show based on her daily life. The idea for the show was to have a camera crew film Cheyenne for weeks at a time as she pursued her music career.

An agreement was reached and a MTV camera crew started filming in June of 2005.

MTV management was very excited about the show, called "Cheyenne" after its star. "The MTV audience will have a front-row seat to all the struggles and triumphs faced by Cheyenne in her quest to be music's next big star," declared Lois Curren, executive vice-president for MTV Series Entertainment. Cheyenne was seen as a natural fit for the MTV audience because in addition to her career ambitions, she still shares most teenage experiences. "She loves to shop, she's boy crazy, whines about how strict her parents are, hates homework, and is counting the days until she gets her driver's license," Curren said.

The show has no script, other than the prepared narration Cheyenne reads as a voice-over. Cheyenne admits that it was "weird" having the crew around all the time, but "you get used to it after a while. They're like family now, so it's better. I feel more comfortable. But, at first, it's kind of awkward. The first day they were filming, I was really stressed out." The cameras kept running even during family arguments. "My mom and I argue a lot," Cheyenne remarked. "My mom's my manager, my teacher and, of course, my mother. So I guess it gets hard sometimes because we're always around each other."

——— " ———

"My lyrics are not age based," Cheyenne said. "If anything, I write a lot older than my age. Maybe I could outgrow them when I'm more mature, but they are always going to be the songs that introduced me to the world."

——— " ———

The first episode, which aired on May 24, 2006, began with Cheyenne celebrating her 15th birthday the summer before with some Texas friends whom she had not seen for a while. After a trip to New York City to talk to record executives, Cheyenne traveled to Los Angeles for a concert, where she battled a sore throat and a bad case of nerves. Subsequent episodes showed Cheyenne breaking up with a boyfriend, moving to California with her parents, going on tour, getting a new boyfriend, shooting a music video, and performing with her musical idol, Sheryl Crow.

When Cheyenne watches the show, she admits that she sometimes has to pinch herself in excitement to relive all that has happened to her. "I'll have one of those, 'oh, my gosh, that's hysterical, that's me' moments," she said. Other times, she winces in embarrassment at the TV screen. In one episode, for instance, "I'm picking a wedgie," she said. "I could change it if I really wanted to, if I was like 'please don't put that in there,' and they wouldn't, or we would compromise, but I know that it's reality and I know that they're trying to be real, so I have to accept the fact that they're going to use that kind of stuff."

On the *Billboard* Charts

The popularity of Cheyenne's MTV television series assured that *The Day Has Come* would receive a fair amount of attention from music fans and critics alike when it was finally released in July 2006. In the first week of its release, *The Day Has Come* appeared on the Billboard 200 list of top-selling albums at number 15. In addition, the song "Hanging On" came in at number 53 on the Billboard Hot 100 singles list. "I feel like I just graduated songwriting school so maybe this album is my diploma," Cheyenne remarked. "I hear a lot of people say that albums are like snapshots in time, but I think my album feels more like a movie because I see myself growing up in these songs."

> *Cheyenne's song "Hanging On" became a hit single for the young singer. "It's a song about following your dreams and never letting things stand in your way; basically what I've been doing all my life," Cheyenne explained. "The song was really important to me because it kept reminding me to be patient, which is something that I'm not very good at."*

The Day Has Come was embraced by fans of Cheyenne's television show. But music critics gave it mixed reviews. Some reviewers admitted that Cheyenne displayed talent, but they also asserted that the album was bland and uninspired. Other reviewers, including Stephen Thomas Erlewine of the website allmusic.com, had a more positive assessment. "[Cheyenne] still sounds like a teen, but that's the good thing about *The Day Has Come*: it has the musical scope of somebody in their early twenties, but the freshness and spunk of a teenager, which is quite remarkable," wrote Erlewine. "So maybe she did get an unfair advantage by being plastered all over MTV prior to the release of her debut, but this record is good enough to provide a compelling reason why Epic and MTV have staked so much on Cheyenne Kimball: based on this very good debut, she certainly does seem the star she's positioned to be."

Cheyenne performing at a party for her debut album, The Day Has Come, *2006.*

Cheyenne's popularity with American teens has led several companies to approach her about endorsing their products. Cheyenne has appeared in a series of television and print advertisements with the 1980s rock star Pat Benatar for a special vintage collection of the Candie's brand of apparel, footwear, and fashion accessories. Cheyenne has also signed on to represent the Sephora cosmetic company in advertisements for its line of "Piiink" makeup.

HOME AND FAMILY

When she is not on tour, Cheyenne lives with her parents in Los Angeles. Her mother travels with Cheyenne and aims to keep her "in my sight at all times. . . . to protect her from this business. She calls the shots but also she's still a 16-year-old who was only allowed to start dating this year, isn't going to be allowed to play bars until she's of age and gets grounded with no computer access frequently." Cheyenne has two black teacup chihuahuas that are named Olivia and Priscilla. "They are very spoiled!" she said.

HOBBIES AND OTHER INTERESTS

Cheyenne has a blog on MySpace.com, which she updates frequently to keep her fans up to date on her touring schedule and other activities. In her spare time, she also enjoys shopping and reading (her favorite books are the "Gossip Girls" series). To keep herself in shape, Cheyenne tries to work out five times a week.

SELECTED CREDITS

Recordings

The Day Has Come, 2006

Television

"Cheyenne," 2006-

FURTHER READING

Periodicals

Boston Herald, May 29, 2006, p.O24
Dallas Morning News, Jan. 2, 2006, p.B1
Fresno (CA) Bee, June 22, 2006, p.E1
Girls' Life, June/July 2006, p.36; Oct./Nov. 2006, p.38
Hartford (CT) Courant, Aug. 17, 2006, Calendar p.11
New Jersey Star-Ledger, Aug. 9, 2006, p.34
Toronto Sun, June 25, 2005, p.S20

Online Articles

http://www.ellegirl.com/article/article.do?articleId=5230
   (*ELLEgirl,* "Cheyenne Kimball: On the Verge," Aug. 20, 2006)
http://www.teenmag.com/celeb/babe/articles/0,,639409_688920,00.html
   (*Teenmag,* "Getting to Know: Cheyenne," undated)
http://bellaonline.com/ArticlesP/art42310.asp
   (*BellaOnline,* "Cheyenne Kimball Interview," undated)
http://www.billboard.com/bbcom/search/google/article_display.jsp?vnu
   _content_id=1002877080
   (*Billboard,* "Cheyenne Kimball," July 20, 2006)

ADDRESS

Cheyenne Kimball
Epic Records
Sony BMG Music Entertainment
550 Madison Avenue
New York, NY 10022-3211

WORLD WIDE WEB SITES

http://www.cheyennemusic.com
http://www.mtv.com/ontv/dyn/cheyenne/series.jhtml

Barack Obama 1961-

American Political Leader
U.S. Senator from Illinois

BIRTH

Barack Obama, known in childhood as Barry, was born on August 4, 1961, in Honolulu, Hawaii. His mother was Stanley Ann Dunham, a teacher and anthropologist. She was given her unusual first name by her father, who had hoped for a son; she eventually dropped the name Stanley and was known simply as Ann. Obama is named after his father, Barack Obama Sr., who was a Kenyan government official. Obama has eight half-siblings, including one half-sister from his mother's second marriage and seven half-brothers and half-sisters from his father's first and third marriages.

YOUTH

Obama's father came to the United States on an education scholarship from a small village in Kenya, a country located on the eastern coast of Africa. The Kenyan government sponsored Obama Sr.'s college education in America in exchange for a promise that he return to Kenya and work for the government after completing his studies. Obama Sr. left his Kenyan wife and children behind and traveled to Hawaii in 1958, where he became the first African to attend the University of Hawaii in Honolulu. It was there that he met Obama's mother, Ann Dunham.

Despite their different backgrounds, Obama Sr. and Dunham quickly fell in love and decided to marry. Marriage between a white woman and a black man, however, was not socially accepted in the late 1950s—an era in which many white Americans openly embraced racial segregation and bigoted views. In fact, marriage between people of different races was a felony crime in many states; some state laws called for extended jail sentences or even death for people convicted of such an offense. These feelings and discriminatory laws were especially common in the Deep South, but they existed throughout the country.

"It was women," wrote Obama, "who provided the ballast in my life—my grandmother, whose dogged practicality kept the family afloat, and my mother, whose love and clarity of spirit kept my sister's and my world centered."

Hawaii, though, was different. Its society was made up of people from many different races, including native Hawaiians, Asians, Filipinos, Portuguese, African-Americans, and whites. People living in Hawaii were generally more accepting of racial differences than residents of other parts of the United States. This environment made it easier for Obama's parents to marry.

When Obama was born, the new family lived together with Ann's parents, Stanley and Madelyn Dunham, in a small apartment near the university. Obama's grandparents often cared for him while his parents attended classes. In 1963, when he was two years old, his father left Hawaii to continue his studies at Harvard University in Cambridge, Massachusetts.

Obama and his mother stayed in Hawaii because the scholarship provided to Obama Sr. did not include enough money to support the whole family. They divorced a short time later. Obama's father then returned to Kenya and took a government position, fulfilling his obligation to the Kenyan government that had paid for his education.

Obama thus grew up without his father. He notes that as he grew older, his mother remained in regular contact with his father, and older men such as a stepfather and his maternal grandfather gave him guidance and affection. But as he wrote in *The Audacity of Hope,* "it was women . . . who provided the ballast in my life — my grandmother, whose dogged practicality kept the family afloat, and my mother, whose love and clarity of spirit kept my sister's and my world centered."

——— **"** ———

"[Living in Jakarta] left a very strong mark on me . . . because you got a real sense of just how poor folks can get," Obama recalled. "You'd have some army general with 24 cars and if he drove one once then eight servants would come around and wash it right away. But on the next block, you'd have children with distended bellies who just couldn't eat."

——— **"** ———

From Hawaii to Indonesia

Obama spent his early childhood in a Hawaiian paradise, exploring beautiful beaches, learning to swim and body surf in the ocean, and going on excursions with his grandfather. He was exposed to all different cultures during visits with his grandfather's friends. He learned to enjoy traditional Hawaiian poi (a sticky grayish-purple pudding made from pounded taro, a root plant related to the potato), sashimi (thinly sliced raw fish), and rice candy with edible wrappers. His mother and grandparents often told stories about his father so that Obama would know about him.

When Obama was six years old, his life changed dramatically. His mother married an Indonesian man named Lolo, another foreign student whom she met at the University of Hawaii. In 1967 Obama and his mother moved to Jakarta, Indonesia, an island nation in Southeast Asia. Trading Honolulu city life and the ocean for an open-walled house on the edge of the jungle, Obama soon adapted to his new life. He had a large ape named Tata for a pet, along with a big yellow dog. The household also included large colorful tropical birds, including a white cockatoo and two birds of paradise, chickens and ducks that wandered freely outside the house, and two baby crocodiles that lived in a pond in a corner of the yard.

Lolo taught Obama how to box, and the youngster learned to eat native foods like raw green chili peppers, dog meat, snake meat, and roasted grasshopper, which Obama later remembered only as "crunchy." Obama slept under a mosquito net, falling asleep to the sounds of the jungle each night. In his autobiography *Dreams from My Father*, he described these years as "one long adventure, the bounty of a young boy's life."

During his years in Jakarta, however, Obama also became aware of poverty and human despair for the first time. Most Indonesians in the area were farmers who were at the mercy of the weather, which

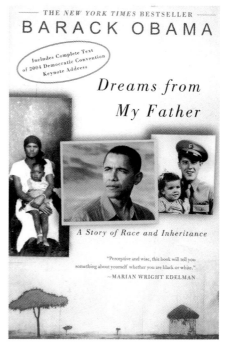

Obama recounts his family background and early life in his memoir, Dreams from My Father.

was notoriously severe and unpredictable in that part of the world. Sometimes it rained so much that crops were washed away in rivers of mud, while other times drought conditions would turn the fields as hard as stone. Many people struggled just to survive from day to day, and beggars frequently came to his house asking for help, food, or money. "It left a very strong mark on me living there because you got a real sense of just how poor folks can get," Obama recalled. "You'd have some army general with 24 cars and if he drove one once then eight servants would come around and wash it right away. But on the next block, you'd have children with distended bellies who just couldn't eat."

Obama also had his first realizations about race and racial differences in Jakarta. When he was about seven years old, he was waiting at his mother's office for her to get out of a meeting. Idly paging through a magazine, he found a story about African-American people who had tried to bleach their skin in order to appear white. The results of the bleaching procedure were terrible, and the photos showed strange-looking people who seemed very sad. Obama recalled feeling angry and confused by the pictures. "I remember that was the first time when I thought about race not in terms of me being darker than somebody else, but in terms of thinking, 'You know, there's something about race that's not a good thing.' I didn't think of it in terms of being about my own race necessarily, but it struck me that there was this sickness out there that would cause somebody to feel they had to bleach their skin."

Up until that point, Obama had not thought much about race, or the idea that he might be different somehow from his mother and grandparents. The magazine pictures disturbed him so deeply that he felt unable to talk to anyone about how he felt. It would be many years before he was able to make any sense of the swirl of emotions he felt on that day.

Returning to Hawaii

Many Americans living in Jakarta were business executives or government officials. Most of them enrolled their children in an international school in the city. Obama, though, attended a school with mostly Indonesian students. His mother supplemented his education with lessons at home. She woke Obama at four o'clock each morning for several hours of study before school.

When Obama was ten years old, his mother decided that she could better prepare him for the future by enrolling him in a school back in the United States. She thus sent him back to Hawaii to live with his grandparents while she remained in Jakarta. In 1971 he enrolled in Punahou Academy, a prestigious school that began with fifth grade and continued through high school.

Obama recalled his early days at Punahou as "a ten-year-old's nightmare." Because life in Hawaii was so drastically different from the village in Jakarta, Obama was unprepared for traditional schooling. His clothes were old-fashioned and dowdy, he did not know how to play football or ride a skateboard like the other kids, and none of them knew how to play soccer, badminton, or chess. He was also one of only a few African-American students in the whole school, and he began to be painfully conscious of his race. Other students teased him about his name, his hair, and his African heritage.

Desperate to defend himself from this harassment, Obama made up stories about his background to impress the other kids. He claimed that his father was an African prince and the chief of his tribe, and that he himself would one day become the chief when the time was right. These tales, combined with Obama's winning smile and charisma, brought an end to the teasing. By the time he entered high school, he was actually one of the more popular students in his class.

Obama's first year back in Hawaii was also highlighted by a month-long visit from his father. He found his father to be both intimidating and fascinating. He was especially interested in his father's descriptions of his own childhood and of African culture in general. The month passed quickly, and Obama's father then returned to Kenya. The two never saw each other again.

Searching for Identity

By the time that Obama entered high school at Punahou, his mother had separated from Lolo. She returned to Honolulu and began studying for a master's degree in anthropology. Obama left his grandparents' apartment and went to live nearby with his mother and his half-sister Maya. He joined the high school basketball team, made fairly good grades, and took part-time jobs to make extra money.

During this time, though, Obama struggled privately with issues of race and his own biracial background. He loved the white family members that surrounded him at home, and he established strong friendships with a few African-American friends at school, but Obama felt like an outsider in both communities. Many fellow African-American students at the school believed that all whites were racist, and when he challenged these claims he was ridiculed. Although he had always enjoyed support and love from his family, Obama stopped telling people that his mother was white.

> *"I learned to slip back and forth between my black and white worlds," Obama said. "Sometimes I lashed out at white people and sometimes I lashed out at black people. I knew there had to be a different way for me to understand myself as a black man and yet not reject the love and values given to me by my mother and her parents."*

As a teenage boy trying to find his place in the world, Obama says that he "learned to slip back and forth between my black and white worlds. . . . Sometimes I lashed out at white people and sometimes I lashed out at black people. I knew there had to be a different way for me to understand myself as a black man and yet not reject the love and values given to me by my mother and her parents. I had to reconcile that I could be proud of my African-American heritage and yet not be limited by it."

79

Obama with his paternal grandmother in Kenya.

During this time, Obama began to read works by such African-American authors as James Baldwin, Toni Morrison, Malcolm X, Ralph Ellison, Langston Hughes, W.E.B. DuBois, and Richard Wright. He gained some understanding of race relations and self-identity from studying these writers, but still felt caught in the middle of two opposing communities. By the late 1970s, though, he reached a greater level of comfort with his heritage. During this time, Obama realized that no matter what his racial background was, he would always be seen as African American. "If I was an armed robber and they flashed my face on television, they'd have no problem labeling me as a black man," he said. "So if that's my identity when something bad happens, then that's my identity when something good happens as well." Eventually much of Obama's frustration, confusion, and self-doubt subsided, although he still felt like an outsider among other African Americans.

EDUCATION

Obama's first few years of schooling were at a public school in Jakarta, but at age 10 he was sent to Hawaii so that he could receive his education in an American school. He attended Punahou Academy in Honolulu and earned his high school diploma in 1979. Later that same year, Obama enrolled in Occidental College in Los Angeles, California, where he studied international law, economics, and social issues.

At Occidental, Obama became part of a larger African-American community for the first time. He was active in the Black Students Association, and spent many hours discussing philosophy and literature with his friends. Around this time he stopped telling people his name was Barry, and began using Barack, his full name.

Becoming a Political Activist

Obama also participated in student demonstrations and rallies on a variety of issues during his time on the Occidental campus. He worked particularly hard on the issue of apartheid in South Africa, a country located at the southernmost tip of the continent of Africa. Apartheid, meaning "apartness" in the South African Africaans language, was a social and political policy of racial segregation and discrimination that was enforced by white minority governments in South Africa from 1948 to 1994. During the 1980s, the South African government came under tremendous pressure to end apartheid. This unrelenting pressure from student activists, human rights organizations, and governments around the world forced South Africa to officially abolish apartheid in 1994.

Obama's political activism on the apartheid issue sparked his interest in tackling problems in American society as well. He soon discovered that he was a gifted speaker in his own right and that people listened attentively whenever he spoke at a rally or demonstration. "I noticed that people had begun to listen to my opinions," he recalled in *Dreams from My Father.* "It was a discovery that made me hungry for words. Not words to hide behind but words that could carry a message, support an idea."

Living in New York City

In 1981 Obama took advantage of a college transfer program and enrolled at Columbia University in New York City. He wanted to experience life in what he considered to be a "true city, with black neighborhoods in close proximity." Obama spent all his free time walking the city streets, exploring and observing the exciting world around him. "Manhattan was humming, new developments cropping up everywhere," he recalled. "The beauty, the filth, the noise, and the excess, all of it dazzled my senses; there seemed no constraints on originality of lifestyles." But although Obama enjoyed New York, his studies at Columbia were marred in 1982 by the news that his birth father had died in an automobile accident in Kenya.

Obama graduated from Columbia University in 1983, earning a bachelor's degree in political science. After graduating from college, Obama wanted to work as a community organizer with a nonprofit organization or an African-American elected official. This desire was driven by his belief that the best way to address social problems was to work with local communities. When no one replied to his inquiries, though, he decided to take a more conventional job while he continued his search for the right community work. He worked as a research assistant and financial writer in New York for a consulting firm that served multinational corporations. But when he became concerned that he was drifting away from his dream of community work, Obama quit his job and took a series of positions with various political campaigns in New York and surrounding areas.

——— " ———

"I noticed that people had begun to listen to my opinions," Obama recalled in **Dreams from My Father.** *"It was a discovery that made me hungry for words. Not words to hide behind but words that could carry a message, support an idea."*

——— " ———

Most of these jobs were volunteer positions, or paid very little money. Obama paid for his living expenses out of the money he had saved. By 1985 his savings were almost gone and he was reluctantly considering a return to the corporate world. At that time, though, he was offered a job with an organization in Chicago. He accepted the position, which set him on a new and exciting path in his life.

Moving to Chicago

As a community organizer for Chicago's Developing Communities Project, Obama worked with some of the poorest neighborhoods on the south side of Chicago. "I took a chance and it paid off," he said. "It was probably the best education I've ever had." He led a coalition of ministers and volunteers who pushed for improved living conditions in neighborhoods that were plagued by crime and high unemployment. He also helped to form a ten-

Obama as a law student at Harvard in 1990, shortly after being elected president of the Harvard Law Review.

ants' rights group in some of Chicago's poorest housing projects, and he established a job training program to help unemployed people in the area.

Obama then decided that studying the law would help him understand how to implement social change on a larger scale. He wanted to learn about "power's currency," things like economics, legislation, business and financial regulations, and real estate. Believing that deep knowledge of these topics would help him to be more effective at helping others, Obama left Chicago to attend Harvard Law School in Cambridge, Massachusetts. Besides being one of the most prestigious universities in the country, it was also the school that his father had attended many years earlier.

Before starting classes at Harvard, though, Obama made his first journey to Kenya, where he met his extended family from his father's side for the first time. As he traveled from Nairobi to the surrounding villages, Obama learned more about his father and his African heritage. This trip allowed Obama to explore a side of himself from which he had always felt disconnected. He was also able to resolve the feelings of abandonment that had been with him since he was a young boy. Being welcomed into his father's family gave Obama the sense of belonging that he had been looking for his whole life.

Making Waves at Harvard

Obama entered Harvard in 1988. At the end of his first year there, he won a place on the *Harvard Law Review*, a legal journal run entirely by students. The *Harvard Law Review* is considered to be the most prestigious of all law reviews in the country, and election to its staff is the highest honor for law students. Obama was one of 80 student editors who prepared articles for the monthly journal. After only one year on the staff, Obama was elected by all the other editors as president of the *Review* in 1990. He was the first African American to receive this honor in the 120-year history of the *Harvard Law Review*.

The presidency of the *Harvard Law Review* assured that Obama would have his choice of high-profile jobs after graduation. Many law review presidents go on to highly sought-after clerkships with the U.S. Supreme Court, or else they can choose from multiple offers to work at law firms across the country. Obama chose neither of these options. After graduation, he planned to work for a corporate law firm for a short time, return to community work, and then explore a life in politics. "One of the luxuries of going to Harvard Law School is it means you can take risks in your life," Obama said. "You can try to do things to improve society and still land on your feet. That's what a Harvard education should buy — enough confidence and security to pursue your dreams and give something back."

Many of the students and faculty members at Harvard had no doubt that Obama would be successful in politics. Professor Laurence Tribe, one of the country's best-known attorneys, taught Obama constitutional law and chose him as a research assistant. He was dazzled by Obama's potential. "I've known senators, presidents," he told *Time* magazine. "I've never known anyone with what seems to me more raw political talent."

The summer before he graduated, Obama returned to Chicago to work as a clerk in a large law firm. Although he came to dislike the corporate environment of the firm, he realized during that summer that Chicago was his home. He decided to return to Chicago after completing his law degree. Obama graduated from Harvard Law Schol in 1991 with highest honors.

CAREER HIGHLIGHTS

Obama's first work in Chicago after graduating was as a lawyer specializing in civil rights. In 1992 he directed Illinois Project Vote, which registered 150,000 new voters. One year later, he began teaching constitutional law at the University of Chicago. In his spare time, Obama began writing his autobiography. He recognized that he was really only just beginning his ca-

Obama filing petitions with the State Board of Elections to get on the ballot for the race for a seat in the U.S. Senate.

reer and rather young to be writing his life story, but he felt that he had some valuable things to say. "By writing about my mistakes, I was trying to show how I was vulnerable to the same pitfalls as American youth everywhere." *Dreams from My Father* was published in 1995.

Entering Politics

In 1996 Obama ran for a seat in the Illinois state legislature as a member of the Democratic Party and won the election. Four years later, his bid for a seat in the U.S. House of Representatives was turned back in the primary election by Democratic incumbent Bobby Rush. But this defeat did not deter Obama. Instead, he returned to Illinois state government and compiled an impressive record of legislative success. In 2003, for example, he successfully pushed for a new Illinois state law that required law enforcement agencies to make recordings of police interrogations and confessions in homicide cases. Overall, Obama ushered 26 bills through the Illinois state legislature, including a large tax credit for the working poor and expanded health care benefits for uninsured children and adults. He also cosponsored legislation to prevent racial profiling by requiring all Illinois police departments to report the race of every person stopped for questioning for any reason.

In 2004 Obama launched a campaign for the Democratic nomination for an open seat in the U.S. Senate representing Illinois. Obama secured the nomination, partly because of his charisma and thoughtful analysis of the issues, and partly because of damaging revelations about the personal life of his leading opponent. After his victory in the primary election, Obama said, "I think it is fair to say the conventional wisdom was we could not win. We didn't have enough money. We didn't have enough organization. There was no way that a skinny guy from the South Side with a funny name like Barack Obama could ever win a statewide race. Sixteen months later we are there."

——— **"** ———

"There's not a liberal America and a conservative America, there is the United States of America," Obama declared in his famous 2004 Democratic Convention address. *"There's not a black America and a white America and Latino America and Asian America, there is the United States of America."*

——— **"** ———

But winning the primary meant that Obama's work was only just beginning. He still had to run a successful campaign against Republican candidate Jack Ryan to win the Senate seat. In a remarkable turn of events, though, Ryan was forced to withdraw from the race due to a public scandal. It took the Republican Party nearly four months of valuable campaign time to find a replacement candidate. During this time, meanwhile, Obama connected with Illinois voters who were inspired by his hopeful and patriotic campaign themes.

Speaking at the Democratic National Convention

By the summer of 2004, Obama's soaring popularity had caught the attention of national Democratic leaders. Eager to showcase the exciting young politician, they asked him to give the keynote address at the 2004 Democratic National Convention in Boston, Massachusetts. The keynote speech is an honor usually reserved for the most respected and seasoned politicians, so it was highly unusual to select a state legislator who had not yet been elected to Congress for the role. Undaunted by any of this, Obama accepted the invitation and wrote his speech during two nights in hotel rooms while he was traveling for his own campaign. The eloquent speech he delivered at the convention has been called one of the greatest convention speeches of all time.

Obama giving the keynote speech at the 2004 Democratic National Convention.

Obama's address was both humble and inspiring. It praised America as truly a land of opportunity, declaring that "I stand here knowing that my story is part of the larger American story, that I owe a debt to all those who came before me, and that, in no other country on earth, is my story even possible." But he observed that America would never achieve its fullest potential if it was unable to overcome the distrust and prejudices that divide many Americans. "There's not a liberal America and a conservative America, there is the United States of America. There's not a black America and a white America and Latino America and Asian America, there is the United States of America. . . . Go to any inner city neighborhood, and folks will tell you that government alone can't teach our kids to learn — they know that parents have to teach, that children can't achieve unless we raise their expectation and turn off the television sets and eradicate the slander that says a black youth with a book is acting white."

Obama put into words what many people had been thinking and feeling, and his remarks resonated with the convention crowd and television viewers alike. By the next morning, he had become an instant celebrity, the political equivalent of a rock star. Requests for interviews, talk show appearances, and speaking engagements flooded into his office. Reflecting on his newfound fame, Obama acknowledged that "the news coverage was very flattering. But the best sign came when we were walking down the street in Boston and the hotel doormen and the cops and the bus drivers were saying, 'Good speech.' It's when you know you've gone beyond the political insiders. . . . I didn't realize then that the speech would strike the chord that it did. I think part of it is that people are hungry for a sense of authenticity. All I was really trying to do was describe what I was hearing on the campaign trail, the stories of the hopes, fears, and struggles of what ordinary people are going through every day."

Obama went on to win the election with an amazing 70 percent of the vote, the widest victory margin for a U.S. Senate seat in Illinois history. He won a majority of votes from virtually every key demographic group. He even won a significant number of votes from Republicans. "I debunked this notion that whites won't vote for blacks," he said. "Or suburbanites won't vote for city people. . . . People may look different, talk different, and live in different places, but they've got some core values that they all care about and they all believe in. If you can speak to those values, people will respond — even if you have a funny name."

————— " —————

"People may look different, talk different, and live in different places, but they've got some core values that they all care about and they all believe in," Obama declared. "If you can speak to those values, people will respond — even if you have a funny name."

————— " —————

Becoming a Senator

With his election triumph, Obama became the only African American serving in the U.S. Senate, the third in the last 100 years, and the fifth ever in the history of the U.S. Congress. The national media referred to these facts repeatedly, but Obama was careful to note that the people of Illinois had elected a senator, not a celebrity. "Given all the hype surrounding my election, I hope people have gotten a sense that I am here to do work and not just chase cameras," he said.

As Obama settled into his new role as a U.S. senator, he set ambitious goals for himself. "I want to make real the American ideal that every child in this country has a shot at life. Right now that's not true. . . . So many kids have the odds stacked so high against them. The odds don't have to be that high. . . . There are things we can afford to do that will make a difference." He also restated his intentions to try to tear down walls of distrust

Sen. Obama testifies alongside Sen. John McCain during a 2006 meeting of the Senate Homeland Security Committee.

and animosity between ethnic, religious, and social groups in America. "I'm well situated to help the country understand how we can both celebrate our diversity in all its complexity and still affirm our common bonds," he said. "We have to build a society on the belief that you are more like me than different from me. That you know your fears, your hopes, your love for your child are the same as what I feel. Maybe I can help with that because I've got so many different pieces in me."

Obama's popularity extended to Kenya, where he is welcomed as a native son. When he visited Kenya in 2006 as part of a tour of several African countries, he was greeted by crowds everywhere he went. Thousands of people lined the streets to watch his motorcade pass by. Across Kenya, schools, roads, and even babies have been named after him. Obama took maximum advantage of his celebrity status. For example, he repeatedly spoke out on the issue of AIDS, which has devastated many Kenyan communities and families. At one point he even went to a public clinic and submitted to an AIDS test himself as a way of raising public awareness and encouraging Kenyans to be tested for the AIDS virus.

The Audacity of Hope

In 2006 Obama published his second book, *The Audacity of Hope: Thoughts on Reclaiming the American Dream.* His purpose in writing this work, he explained, was to help Americans reclaim a sense of pride, duty, solidarity, and shared sacrifice — things that he worries are being lost in a sea of political ruthlessness, economic uncertainty, and fears about the future. "I offer no unifying theory of American government," he wrote. "Instead what I offer is something more modest: personal reflections on those values and ideals that have led me to public life, some thoughts on the ways that our current political discourse unnecessarily divides us, and my own best assessment — based on my experience as a senator and lawyer, husband and father, Christian and skeptic — of the ways we can ground our politics in the notion of a common good."

Obama said his goal in writing The Audacity of Hope *was to share "my own best assessment — based on my experience as a senator and lawyer, husband and father, Christian and skeptic — of the ways we can ground our politics in the notion of a common good."*

Obama's hopeful and encouraging message resonated with American readers, who quickly pushed the book to the top of bestseller lists around the country. It also was warmly received by many reviewers.

Looking to the Future

Obama's own future has been the subject of much public commentary and discussion. Although he has spent relatively few years in national politics, many political analysts have predicted that he could become the first African-American U.S. President. They point to his popularity and his unique ability to gain support from all kinds of people as evidence that he might one day occupy the White House. For his part, Obama insists that he is focused on his responsibilities as a U.S. senator. But he has not ruled out the possibility of a run for the presidency in 2008.

In his daily life Obama is inspired by such heroes as Abraham Lincoln, Martin Luther King Jr., Indian political and spiritual leader Mahatma Ghandi, and Mexican-American labor leader Cesar Chavez. Although each worked on different causes, in different places and times, they all believed in bringing about change through peaceful means. Obama describes them as "people who struggled not only with right vs. wrong but right vs. right. They struggled with values that are difficult and contradictory. . . . They didn't just practice politics. They changed how people thought about themselves and each other. . . . They dug really deep into the culture and wrestled with it." These are the ideals that Obama keeps in mind for his own work.

Obama's talents as a powerful speaker remain in high demand. He spends a significant amount of time campaigning for other Democratic candidates who are running for various offices, and he makes appearances all over the country whenever his schedule permits. Obama sees these opportunities as another way that he can work to create unity and bring about change. "I feel confident that if you put me in a room with anybody — black, white, Hispanic, Republican, Democrat — give me half an hour and I will walk out with the votes of most of the folks. . . . I don't feel constrained by race, geography, or background in terms of making a connection with people."

MARRIAGE AND FAMILY

Obama met his wife Michelle Robinson in Chicago. They married in 1992 and have two daughters, Malia Ann (born 1999) and Natasha (born 2002). Michelle works as an executive in the University of Chicago Hospital system.

Obama divides his time between Washington DC and Chicago. He works during the week in Washington and returns to Chicago each weekend to be with his family. "The hardest thing about the work I do is the strain it puts on Michelle, and not being around enough for the kids," he said. When he is home, he strives to lead a normal life. In his free time, he likes to read, take walks, and go to the movies. His household chores include taking out the garbage and grocery shopping.

WRITINGS

Dreams from My Father, 1995
The Audacity of Hope: Thoughts on Reclaiming the American Dream, 2006

HONORS AND AWARDS

One of the Fifty Most Intriguing Blacks of 2004 (*Ebony*): 2004
Newsmaker of the Year (National Newspaper Publishers Association): 2004
Grammy Award: 2005, Best Spoken Word Album for *Dreams from My Father*
Image Awards (NAACP): 2005 (two awards), Fight for Freedom Award, Chairman's Award
One of the 100 Most Influential People (*Time*): 2005

FURTHER READING

Books

Brill, Marlene Targ. *Barack Obama: Working to Make a Difference,* 2006
Contemporary Black Biography, Vol. 49, 2005
Obama, Barack. *Dreams from My Father,* 1995
Obama, Barack. *The Audacity of Hope,* 2006

Periodicals

American Prospect, Feb. 2006, p.22
Black Enterprise, Oct. 2004, p.88
Chicago Tribune, Mar. 20, 2005, p.C1; June 30, 2005
Current Biography Yearbook, 2005
Ebony, Nov. 2004, p.196
Jet, Aug. 16, 2004, p.4; Apr. 11, 2005, p.30
Nation, June 26, 2006
National Journal, Mar. 18, 2006, p.18
New York Times, Oct. 25, 2004, p.A4
New Yorker, May 31, 2004
Newsweek, Dec. 27, 2004, p.74; Sep. 11, 2006, p.26
O: The Oprah Magazine, Nov. 2004, p.248
Rolling Stone, Dec. 30, 2004, p.88
Time, Nov. 15, 2004, p.74; Oct. 23, 2006, p.44
USA Today, Mar. 6. 2006, p.A1

Online Databases

Biography Resource Center Online, 2006, article from *Contemporary Authors Online,* 2006

ADDRESS

Sen. Barack Obama
713 Hart Senate Office Building
Washington, DC 20510

WORLD WIDE WEB SITES

http://obama.senate.gov
http://www.barackobama.com

Soledad O'Brien 1966-

American Journalist
Co-Host of the CNN Daily News Program
"American Morning"

BIRTH

Maria de la Soledad Teresa O'Brien was born on September 19, 1966. She grew up in St. James, New York, a small suburban town on the north shore of Long Island. Her full first name is a common one among Hispanic Catholic families. It translates as "Our Lady of Solitude," a title honoring the

Virgin Mary. Even as a small child, however, she answered to the shortened version, "Soledad," and the nickname "Solly."

Her father, Edward O'Brien, is a professor of mechanical engineering at the State University of New York at Stony Brook. Her mother, Estella, worked as a high school teacher for many years before retiring. Soledad was the fifth of six siblings. Her eldest sister, Maria, was born in 1961; Cecilia followed in 1962; older brother Tony was born in 1963, followed by another sister, Estela, in 1964. Soledad also has a younger brother, Orestes, who was born in 1968.

YOUTH

O'Brien's parents met in the late 1950s as students at Johns Hopkins University in Baltimore, Maryland. Her father was from Toowoomba, Australia, and had an Irish background, while her mother was from Cuba and of African and Spanish descent. When the two decided to marry, they had to go to Washington DC to do so, because marriage between people of different races was illegal in Maryland at that time.

After marrying, the O'Briens moved to St. James, New York, in hopes of finding a more tolerant atmosphere in which to raise their children. They found what they were looking for, but even so, "when you are the only Cuban black family in town it is strange," Soledad said. "You stick out." O'Brien insists that she never felt traumatized by the ethnic differences between her family and the rest of the community. But she also grew up convinced she would "never date anybody in high school. Nobody wants to date somebody who looks different," she recalled.

EDUCATION

Soledad and her siblings were all energetic, competitive students who loved school. Their parents, both educators, strongly encouraged their children to learn and made it clear that college was a top priority. All six of the O'Brien children eventually attended Harvard University in Cambridge, Massachusetts, either as undergraduates or in graduate school. From there they pursued rewarding careers in business, medicine, and law. Soledad was successful as well, but her education choices prepared her for a different career path.

After graduating from Smithtown High School East in St. James, New York, O'Brien enrolled at Harvard. "I met a lot of international students and people with ideas from A to Z," she remembered. "I felt comfortable in my skin, seeing that everybody did what they wanted to do and were happy." O'Brien knew that she wanted to get into a profession that would help people, so she first explored a career in the field of medicine. Her struggles with an organic chemistry course, however, convinced her that she did not really have the makings of a true scientist. Rather, she found that she was more interested in the human side of medicine, such as the ways in which individuals and families grappled with health problems or triumphed over life-threatening diseases and other health crises.

During her junior year at Harvard, O'Brien was offered an internship at WBZ, a large Boston television station that was affiliated with the NBC network. "The day I stuck my foot into the newsroom was the day I knew that I was going to be in the business," O'Brien recalled. "It just was one of those moments where you know it's exactly the perfect fit."

Exhilarated by the fast pace and excitement of a big-city newsroom, O'Brien eagerly carried out each task she was asked to do, whether it involved fetching coffee for people or pulling staples out of the wall. "Within about 30 seconds of meeting her, I hoped she would come into television," recalled Jeanne Blake, a producer and medical reporter with the station. "She is one of the brightest people that I have ever met and had almost an instant understanding of the media. Plus she is hysterically funny." For her part, O'Brien says that Blake was an important mentor, one who taught her "to be really obsessed with accuracy, obsessed with detail."

> "The day I stuck my foot into the newsroom was the day I knew that I was going to be in the business," O'Brien recalled. "It just was one of those moments where you know it's exactly the perfect fit."

As it turned out, O'Brien's career path interrupted her studies for several years in the 1990s, when she left school to start work. She later returned to college. In 2000, she received a bachelor's degree in English and American Studies from Harvard.

FIRST JOBS

O'Brien started her first job in television in 1989, when she left behind her studies at Harvard to take a position at WBZ as associate producer and newswriter. She further supplemented her income as the producer of the radio program "Second Opinion" and the creator and host of

"Health Week in Review," both of which aired on the Boston radio station KISS-FM.

In 1991 O'Brien was hired by NBC headquarters in New York City to work as a researcher and field producer for Robert Bazell, the network's medical correspondent. The job gave her valuable experience behind the cameras, but network executives urged her to explore on-air opportunities. In 1993 she relocated from New York to San Francisco to work as a reporter at KRON-TV, the NBC affiliate in that city. Her first live reporting assignment was to cover a major victory by the city's baseball team, the Giants, from a sports bar full of rowdy fans. Just as the cameras rolled, someone from the crowd lunged at her. "[He] grabbed my butt," she explained. "I just stopped talking. Time stopped. The cameraman was going, 'Talk! Talk!'" she recalled. "To this day it makes my skin crawl." When O'Brien was unable to pull her report together, the station cut away to a taped segment.

> O'Brien acknowledges that prejudice remains a problem in America, and that it is always painful to encounter. But she believes that the best thing to do when faced with it is to "move on. You can debate the issues until the cows come home or keep your eyes on the prize."

Unnerved by the incident, O'Brien struggled through her next live appearances. But the station's producers were patient with her, and before long she was delivering live news reports like a seasoned pro. Her assured reporting and likeable screen presence convinced KRON management to promote her to chief of the East Bay news bureau. While employed by the station, she also worked on a Discovery Channel program titled "The Know Zone," winning a local Emmy Award for her contributions to the show. Her personal life, meanwhile, thrived as well. In 1995 she married Bradley Raymond, an investment banker.

During these early years in the television business, O'Brien occasionally was criticized for not being "black enough." In other words, some people felt she should play up the African-American aspect of her background in order to appeal more strongly to African-American viewers. She was even advised to change her name and her appearance, but she never seriously considered following any of this advice. O'Brien's attitude about race and prejudice was formed by her parents. As a biracial couple during the 1950s

O'Brien on the set of "The Site," the MSNBC daily show on technology, 1996.

and 1960s, they often encountered racism and bigotry, but they never let these incidents discourage them from pursuing their dreams.

O'Brien acknowledges that prejudice remains a problem in America, and that it is always painful to encounter. But she believes that the best thing to do when faced with it is to "move on. You can debate the issues until the cows come home or keep your eyes on the prize." Although proud of the African, Hispanic, and Caucasian elements in her background, she ultimately feels that "definitions are important to other people; they make no difference to my life."

CAREER HIGHLIGHTS

O'Brien's career continued to blossom during the mid-1990s, when technological developments were transforming American business and culture in a multitude of ways. The Internet was rapidly evolving from an obscure scientific research tool into a communications network used every day by millions of people and businesses. The technology boom also prompted new business and investment strategies across the United States, including a merger between the Microsoft Corporation and the NBC television network. The new MSNBC cable television network and its partner Web site, msnbc.com, were aimed at young adults who were comfortable with com-

97

puters and technology and eager to stay on the cutting edge of the latest innovations. O'Brien knew she would fit in well with the new network, and in 1996 she left KRON to work for MSNBC.

O'Brien was first slated to host "The Site." One of the first programs planned by MSNBC, it offered the latest in technology news, product reviews, and human interest features for a tech-savvy audience. O'Brien felt she was ideally suited to host this show. Her viewpoint would be the same as that of her viewers—she did not feel threatened by technology, but she was not an expert either. Network executives agreed that she was ideally suited to make the show's tech-heavy subject matter more accessible to a general audience.

O'Brien took the show's subjects seriously, but she also infused the show with a relaxed, humorous quality. When one viewer wrote asking for recommendations on software to make his computer work as an alarm clock, she showed her special brand of lighthearted sarcasm when she told him to "buy an eight-dollar clock at Walgreen's for heaven's sake!" "The Site" and O'Brien quickly gained such a loyal following among technology enthusiasts that she acquired the nickname "Goddess of the Geeks."

Stepping into National News

In 1997 "The Site" was canceled by MSNBC executives who were still looking for the right programming mix for the young network. O'Brien's career was still on the rise, however. She was assigned to host "Morning Blend," a two-hour, weekend news and talk program on MSNBC. Around this same time, she began filling in as co-host on NBC's "Weekend Today" and filing news reports for "NBC Nightly News." She also began making regular appearances on the popular "Today" morning show, either as a substitute host or reporter on breaking news events. "My career has been a history of running with the ball and taking advantage of opportunities," she noted.

O'Brien covered a number of notable news events during this time, including the plane crash that took the life of John F. Kennedy, Jr.; school shootings in Littleton, Colorado and Springfield, Oregon; and the disaster that befell the space shuttle *Columbia*. But not all of the stories she covered were tragic in nature. For example, in 1998 she traveled with Pope John Paul II to Cuba, a Communist country that had never before welcomed a Pope to its shores.

The assignment in Cuba gave O'Brien her first opportunity to visit the country where her mother had been born, and where much of her extended family still lived. She enjoyed meeting her relatives and found the country a beautiful place in some ways, but she was also deeply disturbed by the country's widespread poverty and political repression. "It was a great opportunity. But when I left I got very depressed," she said later. O'Brien nevertheless valued the experience and the insights she gained from it. "Any time you talk about your roots and family, you learn a lot about yourself," she reflected.

In July 1999 O'Brien was named the permanent co-host of "Weekend Today." Her first co-anchor was Jack Ford, who praised his colleague's warmth and professionalism. "With early morning TV, you have to make sure the viewer feels really comfortable with you; Soledad immediately reached a comfort level [with audiences,]" Ford said. After Ford departed the show to work at another network, O'Brien quickly established a good working relationship with his replacement, David Bloom.

Over the next year, O'Brien somehow managed to continue her anchoring duties in New York City while also completing her studies at Harvard. She did so by commuting to her sister's Boston home each Monday, Tuesday, and Wednesday, then returning to New York for work. Moreover, she carried out this hectic, demanding schedule while she was pregnant with her first child. "I'd walk around Harvard Yard thinking, I would pay one of these undergraduates $20 if I could just lie down in her bed for 20 minutes!" she remembered.

> —— **"** ——
>
> *"[Visiting Cuba] was a great opportunity. But when I left I got very depressed,"* O'Brien said. Still, she valued the experience and the insights she gained from it. *"Any time you talk about your roots and family, you learn a lot about yourself."*
>
> —— **"** ——

Weekday News Anchor at CNN

In April 2003, O'Brien's "Weekend Today" co-anchor, David Bloom, unexpectedly died of a pulmonary embolism (a blood clot affecting the lungs) while on assignment in Iraq. He was just 39 years old. "I had looked to David as a role model in many ways," O'Brien said. After he died, she felt that "Weekend Today" ceased to be a team. "The bottom fell out emotionally," she admitted.

O'Brien recognized that it would be easy to remain in what had become a comfortable job and await the designation of a new co-host. But O'Brien said that her colleague's sudden death reminded her that "life is short and

O'Brien on the set of the CNN show "American Morning."

if you have a dream, go out and accomplish it." Accordingly, in July 2003 she accepted an offer from the CNN television news network to co-anchor their weekday morning news show, "American Morning." "I felt like I learned from the best in the business at 'Weekend Today' — Katie Couric and Matt Lauer. I grew. You can't help but grow. But I also learned when to take the next challenge," O'Brien explained.

O'Brien's move to CNN represented a clear step up in her career. It gave her more exposure, more travel opportunities, and more high-profile guests to interview. It also made her more financially secure; her four-year contract with CNN was said to include a salary of approximately $750,000 a year.

Over the next few years, O'Brien's assignments took her all over the world. During these travels, she reported on a fascinating parade of events and people. In the fall of 2003, O'Brien was the only broadcast journalist per-mitted to accompany Laura Bush when the First Lady traveled to Paris and Moscow. In November 2004, she traveled to Columbus, Ohio, to report on disputes over votes cast there in the presidential election. In December of that year she reported from Thailand on the aftermath of the devastating tsunami that took the lives of more than 155,000 people across Southeast Asia. She and her team won the Alfred I. duPont Award for their coverage of that disaster. In July 2005, she reported from London on the terrorist attacks in that city. Later that summer, she went to New Orleans in the wake of Hurricane Katrina to give viewers the story of the storm and the devastating flood that followed it.

O'Brien says that covering these and other world events has given her a global perspective that she wants to pass on to her children. "You just learn so much," she said. "I get to sit there and talk to somebody and be inspired by them. I love to be moved and impressed by people . . . who do remarkable things."

Covering Katrina

O'Brien is frequently characterized as attractive, pleasant, and non-threatening. She has proved her toughness and professionalism, however, on several reporting assignments. In the wake of Katrina, for example, thousands of New Orleans residents were left for days without food, water, medical attention, or adequate police protection. O'Brien seemed to channel the outrage many Americans felt when they saw images of the suffering survivors on television.

In one televised interview, O'Brien confronted Michael Brown, the head of the Federal Emergency Management Agency (FEMA), about the agency's poor response to the disaster. Brown defended himself and FEMA by saying that he had only recently become aware of certain aspects of the situation and stating that communication and travel were difficult in the area. O'Brien promptly challenged these claims: "How is it possible that we're getting better intel [intelligence] than you're getting? We had a crew in the air. We were showing live pictures of the people outside the Convention Center. . . . And also, we've been reporting that officials have been telling people to go to the Convention Center if they want any hope of relief. I don't understand how FEMA cannot have this information." She continued to grill Brown, asking

"Do you look at the pictures that are coming out of New Orleans?" O'Brien demanded in an interview with FEMA Director Michael Brown. "And do you say, I'm proud of the job that FEMA is doing on the ground there in a tough situation? Or do you look at these pictures and you say, this is a mess and we've dropped the ball."

O'Brien reporting from New Orleans after Hurricane Katrina.

why four days had passed without any massive airdrop of food or water to those who were trapped in the Superdome and at the city's Convention Center. "Do you look at the pictures that are coming out of New Orleans?" she demanded. "And do you say, I'm proud of the job that FEMA is doing on the ground there in a tough situation? Or do you look at these pictures and you say, this is a mess and we've dropped the ball."

O'Brien's passion and dedication in covering this story were officially recognized when she and her teammates at CNN were given the George Foster Peabody Award for their reporting on Katrina and the flood in New Orleans. Reflecting on her job and the place of media in society, she stated: "We get to tell people what is happening in the world and be a part of their lives. It is an important mandate and something very valuable."

MARRIAGE AND FAMILY

O'Brien married Bradley Raymond, an investment banker, in 1995. Their first child, Sofia Elizabeth, was born on October 23, 2000; another daughter, Cecilia, followed on March 20, 2002; and the couple welcomed twin boys, Charlie and Jackson, on August 30, 2004. Just as her parents and siblings were very important to her in childhood, so are her husband and children vitally important to her adult life. Working the early morning shift at CNN allows her to be home in time to be involved with her children's daytime activities and at mealtime.

O'Brien's commitment to parenting and strong family bonds is reflected in a bimonthly column she contributes to the magazine *USA Weekend*. Asked about one of the most important things she learned from her own parents about raising children, she said that "it's okay to be strict. That kids, as much as they fight against the rules, they really want them and need them. It takes a lot more time and effort to teach children good manners, but in the long run it is really worth it."

O'Brien is often asked how she manages to balance work with family demands. She says that her secret is "not to strive for real balance. I set a low bar on the things that don't matter, and I set a high bar for the things that do matter—spending lots of time with my kids and husband. It's about being flexible and understanding that we are all human and make mistakes and there are limits to what we can accomplish in 24 hours. Get off your own back!"

> *O'Brien says that she has learned that "it's okay to be strict" as a parent. "Kids, as much as they fight against the rules . . . really want them and need them. It takes a lot more time and effort to teach children good manners, but in the long run it is really worth it."*

O'Brien credits her mother and her three older sisters with showing her that a woman can juggle a fulfilling career and a happy family. The keys, she claims, are learning to prioritize on a daily basis, letting go of the things that are not really essential, and accepting the fact that life doesn't always run smoothly. "Sometimes there's a tsunami and you have to fly to Thailand. Sometimes the first day of school is a priority and you make pancakes and take everyone to school," she said.

HOBBIES AND OTHER INTERESTS

O'Brien likes to hike, swim, and run to stay in shape. She enjoys writing and is working on a book about family and child-raising, as well as a novel loosely based on her mother's life. She also sits on the board of directors of the Harlem School for the Arts.

TELEVISION PROGRAMS

"The Know Zone," 1995
"The Site," 1996-97
"Morning Blend," 1998
"Weekend Today," 1999-2003
"American Morning," 2003-

HONORS AND AWARDS

Hispanic Achievement Award in Communications: 1997
Hispanic Heritage Vision Award (Hispanic Heritage Foundation): 2005
Women of Power Award (National Urban League): 2006
National Association of Minorities in Cable Vision Award: 2006

FURTHER READING

Books

Contemporary Hispanic Biography, Vol.1, 2002
Who's Who in America, 2006

Periodicals

Arizona Republic, Apr. 14, 2006, p.3
Ebony, Dec. 2004, p.8
Electronic Media, June 30, 1997, p.16
Good Housekeeping, Jan. 2006, p.148
Hispanic Outlook in Higher Education, May 17, 2004, p.9
Houston Chronicle, June 17, 2003, p.6
Jet, Dec. 20, 2004, p.26
Latino Leaders, May 1, 2006, p.32
Newsday, June 23, 2005, p.B12
People, June 16, 1997, p.108; May 8, 2000, p.148
Redbook, May 2005, p.29
Runner's World, June 2003, p.18
San Francisco Chronicle, Apr. 15, 1997, p.B1

Online Articles

http://www.hispaniconline.com
   (*Hispanic Magazine,* "And Now the News," June 2001; "Running with
   the News," June 2005)

http://modernmom.com
  (*Modern Mom,* "Modern Mom Profiles . . . CNN's Soledad O'Brien,"
  undated)

Online Databases

Biography Resource Center Online, 2006, article from *Contemporary Hispanic
  Biography,* 2002

ADDRESS

Soledad O'Brien
CNN
One Time Warner Center
New York, NY 10019

WORLD WIDE WEB SITE

http://www.cnn.com

Skip Palenik 1947-
American Forensic Microscope Scientist
World-Renowned Expert in Analysis of Microscopic
Material

BIRTH

Samuel James Palenik III was born in 1947 in Chicago, Illinois.
Palenik was named after his father, who worked as a truck driver, but he has been known by the nickname "Skip" since
early childhood. Palenik's mother was a homemaker. He has
one brother and one sister.

YOUTH

Even as a young boy, Palenik was fascinated by microscopes
and the invisible world they revealed. "The idea of taking a

piece of dust and seeing what others do not see has always intrigued me," he said. "Ever since I was a kid, I've thought there is a whole world of things regular people don't look at."

Palenik's parents encouraged this interest, buying him his first microscope when he was eight years old. "I had wanted it for some time before that, but for Christmas, I got my first one, a Gilbert microscope," he recalled. This microscope could magnify objects up to 400 times their size, and it opened up a whole new world for the inquisitive youngster. Soon he was using the device for hours at a time, studying common items found around the home such as dirt, cooking spices, swatches of clothing, and water.

Palenik also performed all of the experiments outlined in the microscope's instruction manual, which he says may be the most influential book he's ever read. "In the instruction manual, there was a chapter called 'The Vacuum Cleaner Detective,' which was about science and crime detection," he recalled. "It explained how you could take apart your mother's vacuum cleaner bag and decipher all of the components in the dust. I learned how to detect spices from the kitchen, talcum powder from the bathroom, and hairs that belonged to Mom or Dad or my brother or sister. I was hooked. I read everything I could on crime investigation, microscopy, and science. . . . Things just took off from there."

> "I learned how to detect spices from the kitchen, talcum powder from the bathroom, and hairs that belonged to Mom or Dad or my brother or sister," recalled Palenik. "I was hooked. I read everything I could on crime investigation, microscopy, and science. . . . Things just took off from there."

Exploring Laboratory Science

By the time Palenik was 12 years old, his father had built a laboratory for his two sons in the basement of the family's home. Working with his brother Mark, Palenik used the lab to conduct a wide range of scientific experiments. They studied chemical reactions and examined all sorts of household materials, taking samples that would fit under the microscope's lens. The boys also explored basic criminal investigation techniques, such as making marks on sheets of metal with different types of tools in order to study the distinctive marks made by each tool. "We worked through every experiment that I could get supplies for," Palenik said.

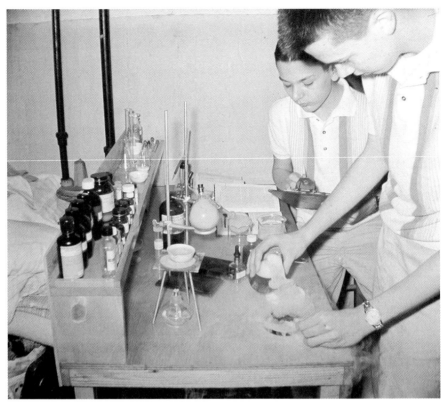

Skip (front) and Mark (rear) in one of their earliest laboratories, about 1955.

The Palenik brothers' experiments led them to make regular trips to the local library and drug store, as well as other places that fed their curiosity. "Our big Saturdays, about once a month, my brother Mark and I would take the Archer Express [train] downtown," Palenik remembered. "There were three stops we would make. The first stop was the Chicago Library reading room. . . . If you got there early, you'd get a seat at those beautiful big tables. We'd sit there all day reading — well, not quite all day, because Mark didn't like that part too much. Then we'd drop off our chemical order at Sargent's Drug Store on Wabash Avenue. A big order for us was $5. We'd saved to get that much to order chemicals for our lab at home. . . . Then we'd go to Kroch's & Brentano's [book store]. I found copies of Charnot and Mason's *Handbook of Chemical Microscopy* in two volumes, and this really opened possibilities. I thought I could do every form of microanalysis with it. Then we'd go to Walgreen's or Woolworth's, where they had a basement cafeteria, and we'd eat lunch. Other Saturdays, we'd do normal kid stuff — go to movies, play ball, or work in our labs."

EDUCATION

Palenik attended elementary and high school in the Chicago area. He recalls that after earning his high school diploma, "I couldn't wait to get to college to study chemistry." But he became discouraged soon after arriving at the University of Illinois at Chicago. His professors tried to steer him away from studying the techniques in which he was most interested. For example, his instructors urged him to reconsider his interest in forensic microscopy, the scientific use of microscopes to examine physical evidence for criminal investigation and other purposes. At the time, researchers had concluded that using microscopes in this way was outdated and would be a useless skill to possess within a matter of a few years. Palenik recalled that one of his professors told him, "This is all very nice, but nobody does this anymore."

—— " ——

"I went back to school for chemistry and was a much better student this time," said Palenik. "I still had my lab, but I paid attention in class more!"

—— " ——

Disheartened by these developments, Palenik drifted away from his classes and launched his own course of study at the university library. Palenik eventually left school and was drafted by the Army in 1966. He served three years in the Army as an intelligence analyst. After completing his military service, Palenik returned to the University of Illinois at Chicago to finish his degree. "I went back to school for chemistry and was a much better student this time. I still had my lab, but I paid attention in class more!" he said. During this time he also worked in various laboratories at the university. Palenik first worked as a research assistant for the Department of Chemistry (1970-1972), then moved on to the Department of Criminal Justice (1972-1974). In 1974, Palenik received his Bachelor of Science (BS) degree in chemistry with an emphasis on analytical methods.

CAREER HIGHLIGHTS

Immediately after graduating from college, Palenik went to work for the McCrone Research Institute in Chicago, a leading research company for law enforcement and criminal investigation agencies around the country. The institute was founded by Walter McCrone, a forensic microscopist who had been one of Palenik's childhood heroes. Palenik had actually contacted McCrone before he had even earned his degree, and it was at that time that the two began a long friendship based on their shared enthusiasm for

Walter McCrone at the microchemical bench in his lab, about 1975.

microscopic science. During the mid-1970s, McCrone was one of the only scientists in the world who remained dedicated to the use of microscopes for investigation and analysis of materials. He became Palenik's mentor, teaching him many advanced research techniques. Under McCrone's tutelage, Palenik declared, "I learned what a real scientist is."

Palenik claims that McCrone deserves special credit for helping him develop and sharpen his skills in logical deduction. In addition to their regular work assignments, the researchers at the McCrone Institute played a never-ending game called "UFO." "You would come into the laboratory in the morning and on your microscope would be a microscope slide, and in a Sharpie pen it said, 'UFO,'" recalled Palenik. "And it could be anything in the world on it. And so we had such things—residue from the bottom of a bag of pistachio nuts . . . combustion products from a cogged railway . . . hops from beer making."

The goal of the game was to correctly identify the material on the slide. Palenik and other lab players would do this by using different microscopes to analyze the material's characteristics, then match those characteristics to a known substance. "Most people think dust is dust," Palenik said. "Well, it's not. It all comes from someplace. It comes from the pollen grains in the air. It comes from fibers. It comes from the asphalt and tire rubber on the roads. Each is a clue to its origin . . . only a microscopist knows what it's like. Dust and debris and stains are our business." The UFO game became Palenik's specialty, and it was valuable in helping him develop his expertise in identifying unknown materials.

Founding Microtrace

When McCrone retired in 1993, Palenik founded his own laboratory called Microtrace. "I always wanted to open my own lab, so people wouldn't touch my stuff," he joked. The Microtrace collection of microscopes can magnify objects up to 70,000 times, using beams of light or streams of electrons to reveal the specific molecular composition of objects. Palenik has also assembled a reference collection of samples of more than 10,000 various materials to use for comparison matching. The collection includes many samples of dust created from drilling, sawing, and crushing different materials. It also includes thousands of different man-made fibers, human and animal hair, pollen, spices, grains, starches, soil, sand, and so on. The Microtrace facility also houses Palenik's large library of books, journals, and specialized encyclopedias. All of these tools are used to characterize and identify unknown materials that are brought to Microtrace for analysis.

——— " ———

"Most people think dust is dust," Palenik said. "Well, it's not. It all comes from someplace. It comes from the pollen grains in the air. It comes from fibers. It comes from the asphalt and tire rubber on the roads. Each is a clue to its origin . . . only a microscopist knows what it's like. Dust and debris and stains are our business."

——— " ———

At Microtrace, Palenik and the other forensic scientists use many different types of microscopes to analyze materials. For example, a comparison microscope is used to compare two materials under exactly the same conditions. A hot stage microscope has a compartment that is temperature controlled by a computer. The temperature can be varied to show the melting point of a particle or fiber. A fluorescence microscope uses an ultraviolet light source instead of visible light commonly used in light microscopes. The ultraviolet radiation is absorbed by certain compounds, which reemit light in the visible wavelength in a process known as fluorescence. This can identify the presence of optical brighteners, dyes, and other organic materials.

Other microscopes in Palenik's investigative arsenal include a reflected light microscope, which is used to study opaque particles. A light source above the specimen focuses on the surface of a sample (like a metallic particle such as lead from a bullet). This can show how light is reflected off the material to reveal striations, cracks, or other markings that give clues about an unknown particle's identity or origin. A scanning electron microscope uses electrons instead of light to create an image. Because an electron has a much shorter wavelength than light in the visible region of the spectrum, a scanning electron microscope sometimes reveals valuable information that is undetectable with a light microscope. Taken together, the results of tests from all these microscopes can reveal many different features of an unknown particle.

————— " —————

"We try to solve problems by establishing facts from the physical evidence we are given," said Palenik. "And usually that evidence is quite small — a grain of sand, a speck of dust. You could probably fit all the material I've been asked to analyze in the last 30 years into a couple of tablespoons."

————— " —————

Crime Scene Investigator

Throughout his career, Palenik has worked on many highly publicized cases on behalf of various clients in the world of law enforcement. He analyzed materials related to the 1993 World Trade Center bombing in New York City and the 1995 bombing of the Alfred P. Murrah Federal Building in Oklahoma City, Oklahoma. Palenik has also helped to determine the source of explosives used in aircraft bombings in Ireland and Japan. He also has participated in the investigation of many serial crimes, including the "Unabomber" mail bombing attacks that claimed three lives and wounded 29 others (Ted Kaczynski was eventually convicted for these bombings, which took place from the late 1970s through the early 1990s) and a series of child murders that terrorized Atlanta from 1979 to 1981 (Wayne Williams was captured and convicted for these crimes in 1982). Palenik also participated in investigations of the terrorist aircraft hijackings and destruction of the World Trade Center towers on September 11, 2001.

Palenik has even lent his expertise to the investigation of crimes of yesteryear. For example, he assisted with a re-investigation of the 1968 assassination of civil rights leader Martin Luther King Jr. This investigation confirmed that King had been shot by only one gunman, contradicting various conspiracy theories.

The fluorescence microscope uses ultraviolet (UV) light, which is absorbed and re-emitted in a process known as fluorescence. It's used in particle analysis and in the study of biological material.

Palenik's talents have drawn the attention of overseas law enforcement agencies as well. The Royal Canadian Mounted Police, England's famed Scotland Yard criminal investigation agency, and the International Criminal Police Organization known as Interpol have all enlisted his help on various cases over the years.

The Search for Truth

Palenik has been hired by both prosecutors and defense attorneys during his long career, but he says that he does not work exclusively for one side or the other. In most cases, in fact, he does not even follow the trial to learn the verdict after he has concluded his research and reported his findings. He simply works to discover, understand, and explain the facts about the material he is asked to analyze. He does recall one time when he happened to hear a news report of a verdict for a trial he'd worked on. "I was real excited," he admitted. "But not for the reason people think, because we caught a killer. It was the intellectual joy a scientist gets from knowing his theory is right. . . . My role is to establish facts. We pick up these little particles, isolate them, analyze them, and finally try and establish what the material is. From there we must take the next step and apply some con-

113

trolled imagination and interpret these findings in the light of the situation. That's justified as long as people know what the facts are and what you are basing your conclusions on. . . . The scientist's role is to establish facts. The jury has to decide who did it."

Even at a time when criminal investigators and courts are increasingly reliant on DNA evidence, cases still arise in which DNA evidence is unavailable. Those are the cases where Palenik's brand of research is most valuable. "We aren't traditional detectives, in that we don't interview suspects and witnesses. Instead, we are true scientific investigators who work in a laboratory with microscopes and chemicals," he observed. "We try to solve problems by establishing facts from the physical evidence we are given," he said. "And usually that evidence is quite small — a grain of sand, a speck of dust. You could probably fit all the material I've been asked to analyze in the last 30 years into a couple of tablespoons."

Palenik pointed to one particular case to show how the smallest piece of evidence can result in an arrest and conviction. His company was called in to investigate an aircraft bombing after other investigators were unable to determine the composition of the bomb, where it came from, or who was responsible for the attack. "We found one particle of cocoa shell dust — used as filler for dynamite — in the bottom of a bag and were able to identify the exact kind of dynamite and trace it back to the suspect's apartment," Palenik recalled. With successes like that, Palenik earned a worldwide reputation as an expert in his field.

Palenik has rejected comparisons to the crime scene investigators featured on the popular television show "CSI," however. "This kind of work isn't what people imagine," he said. "We get facts and go to the library and try to figure out what they mean. Things don't pop out of an instrument. It's not like 'CSI.' . . . If you really want to learn about solving crimes you don't watch 'CSI' — you read Edgar Allan Poe. Anybody who comes to work for me has to read the Poe stories, especially 'The Murders in the Rue Morgue.' They show how to use reason to solve a crime. That's what we do. But to reason you have to have facts. Our laboratory gives you facts."

A Thriving Business

Today, Palenik's skills are in such high demand that he works six or seven days a week. The workload also convinced him to recruit his brother Mark, who joined Microtrace in 2004, and his son Chris, who joined Microtrace one year later. In addition to laboratory research, Palenik sometimes testifies in court in order to explain his findings to the judge, attorneys, and the jury. He is considered an excellent expert witness because his work is thorough and accurate and he is able to communicate facts very well. "You'd think with the work [Palenik] does, he'd be difficult to understand," said Assistant Hennepin County Attorney Mike Furnstahl to the *Chicago Daily Herald.* "But he takes that into account and gives an elementary description. It's not just his expertise, it's the complete lack of bias." That view was echoed by Edward Rhodes of the San Diego police department. "He manages to put things into terms that people who don't have his sophisticated knowledge are able to understand," Rhodes confirmed in an interview with the *Chicago Tribune.*

But Palenik's work is not limited to criminal investigation. He has analyzed art objects and historical documents for scholars and collectors to confirm authenticity and date of creation. He has also performed research for manufacturers of items as varied as beverages, cosmetics, and tobacco products. Sometimes manufacturing companies hire him to analyze the ingredients in a product made by their competitors, and sometimes they want him to look at their own products. Palenik's work has been featured on several programs produced by cable television's History Channel and Discovery Channel, and he has also appeared on the *Oprah* television talk show to explain his analysis of the ingredients used in popular beauty products.

> "You'd think with the work [Palenik] does, he'd be difficult to understand," said Assistant Hennepin County Attorney Mike Furnstahl. "But he takes that into account and gives an elementary description. It's not just his expertise, it's the complete lack of bias."

Palenik revealed that one of his favorite challenges was to analyze Yoo-Hoo, a bottled chocolate drink, to determine why black specks were appearing in their products. Samples had already been analyzed twice, by two different teams of scientists, but they had been unable to agree on what the specks were. One team said the problem was caused by burned milk while the other team insisted that burned sugar was the culprit. Palenik was then called in to investigate. "They thought it was some type of charred material . . . so they sent the sample to me. First, I isolated the specks by chipping away the charred part with microscopic scalpels. Then I tested to see if the particles were a protein or a carbohydrate. . . . Finally, I identified the amino acid that was most prominent—tryptophan, which is highly present in milk but not at all in sugar." Palenik thus confirmed

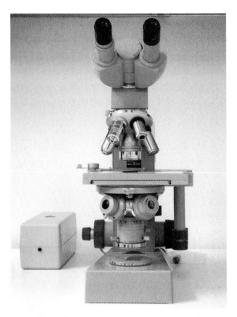

The phase contrast microscope is modified from a normal light microscope to enhance the contrast observed in an image. It's used by biologists and is also used in particle analysis when studying small particles.

the conclusion that the specks were being caused by burned milk during the production process.

In addition to performing microscopic analysis of materials for clients all over the world, Palenik has provided training in his areas of expertise. He has instructed other researchers and law enforcement investigators in microchemical analysis, forensic fiber microscopy, identification of animal hair, and vegetable fiber analysis. Palenik has given classes at the McCrone Institute, where he is a member of the board of directors. He also has taught courses at the Illinois Institute of Technology as well as the University of Illinois at Chicago's School of Pharmacy and Department of Criminal Justice.

Palenik is now recognized as one of only about 24 forensic microscopy experts in the world. He is a member of numerous scientific organizations, including the American Academy of Forensic Sciences, the Canadian Society of Forensic Scientists, and even the International Sand Collectors Society—a valuable source of reference samples for his tests. "I've been looking through a microscope almost every day of my life since I was eight years old," Palenik stated. "I'm one of those people who ended up doing exactly what he always wanted to do. I like to look at something someone has looked at before and see things they've never seen . . . I love it. I am one of the lucky few who is actually doing as an adult what he dreamed about doing as a child. And the job never gets boring."

MAJOR INFLUENCES

Palenik attributes much of his success to the scientists who pioneered the field of forensic microscopy and to the teachers who helped him develop the skills he now uses. In addition to his mentor Walter McCrone, Palenik says that a scientist named Edmond Locard was also very influential. Locard was one of the first forensic microscopists, and he formulated what is now known as the exchange principle: whenever two objects come into contact, there is always a transfer of material. Every person and every object comes into contact with thousands of particles in the course of a day, and microscopic traces of those contacts leave behind a road map of all the places they have been. The science of forensic microscopy is based on Locard's exchange principle, and Palenik is an expert in applying it to form logical, fact-based conclusions.

Palenik's list of heroes also includes the fictional 19th century detective Sherlock Holmes. Holmes is the main character in numerous books and short stories written by Sir Arthur Conan Doyle. Palenik said that he developed a love of Sherlock Holmes stories when he was a young boy, around the same time he became interested in microscopy. Holmes is known for his encyclopedic memory and skills in logical deduction. Like Holmes, Palenik uses scientific reasoning and deduction to make connections and draw conclusions that other investigators might overlook. In fact, Palenik is sometimes compared to his boyhood hero. Peter De Forest, professor of criminalistics at John Jay College of Criminal Justice at the City University of New York, commented in the *Chicago Tribune*, "[Palenik] is the only real-world epitome of Sherlock Holmes. He's a stellar scientist, the kind of guy that Doyle would be writing about if he were writing today. [Palenik] is probably the premier practitioner. He's a top-notch microscopist and problem-solver."

> "
>
> *"I've been looking through a microscope almost every day of my life since I was eight years old," Palenik stated. "I'm one of those people who ended up doing exactly what he always wanted to do. . . . I am one of the lucky few who is actually doing as an adult what he dreamed about doing as a child. And the job never gets boring."*
>
> "

MARRIAGE AND FAMILY

Palenik's wife Peggy is a second-grade teacher. They have two sons, Christopher and Jeffrey. They live in Elgin, Illinois, a suburb of Chicago.

HOBBIES AND OTHER INTERESTS

Palenik has devoted his life to his work, and he has few other interests. His hobbies are collecting, reading, and studying antique books and manuscripts related to microscopic science and microchemistry. His enthusiasm for microscopy has not diminished since he was a boy; in fact, he has admitted that whenever he returns home from a trip, he vacuums his clothes just for fun. He then tries to identify all the particles he finds, working in a custom-built laboratory in the basement of his home. "I stay clear of the lab," said his wife, Peggy. "He doesn't like anyone to touch anything. When you're working with small particles, everything has to be dust free, so you try to keep as few people as possible in the area."

WRITINGS

The Particle Atlas, 1973-1979 (co-author)

FURTHER READING

Periodicals

Chicago, Mar. 2005, p.44
Chicago Tribune, Apr. 7, 1988, p.4; Sep. 6, 1992, p.1, p.6; Dec. 30, 1993, p.3; Apr. 6, 2003, p.10
Los Angeles Times, May 14, 1986, p.4
Odyssey, Jan. 2004, p.35
Reader's Digest, Jan. 2003, p.135

Online Articles

http://www.popsci.com/popsci/crimeseen/982e9aa138b84010vgnvcm100 0004eecbccdrcrd.html
(Popular Science, "Crime Seen," undated)

ADDRESS

Skip Palenik
Microtrace
1750 Grandstand Place
Elgin, IL 60123-4900

WORLD WIDE WEB SITE

http://www.microtracescientific.com

Ivan "Pudge" Rodriguez 1971-

Puerto Rican Professional Baseball Player with the
Detroit Tigers
Record-Setting Catcher with 11 Gold Glove Awards
and 13 All-Star Game Appearances

BIRTH

Ivan Rodriguez was born on November 30, 1971 (some sources
state November 27, 1971) in Manati, Puerto Rico. His father,
Jose Rodriguez, was an electrical supervisor for an international
construction company. His mother, Eva Torres, was a second-

grade teacher, and later became a school principal. Though his parents divorced when he was 12, he has remained close with them both. Ivan has an older brother, Jose Rodriguez Jr., a factory worker and amateur baseball player.

YOUTH

Rodriguez was raised in Vega Baja, Puerto Rico, a town located five miles south of the Atlantic Ocean and 18 miles west of San Juan. He lived in a small cinderblock house in the Algarrobo barrio, a poor neighborhood on the fringe of Vega Baja. At the age of seven, he joined the barrio's little league team and began practicing baseball drills with his father for two or three hours a session.

> *The local baseball field upon which Rodriguez played as a kid had an uneven infield full of pebbles and an outfield with bare patches in the grass. "The ball, it could bounce anywhere," recalled Rodriguez. "It could hit you right in the face. It taught you to be ready for anything."*

Rodriguez loved baseball, and he often dreamed of becoming a major league pitcher. After school and throughout the summer, he walked through the neighborhood with a bat and ball, looking for kids with whom he could play. The equipment he used was battered and worn, but he never let that bother him. He and his brother made baseballs by wrapping medical tape around a cork, and they often played a baseball-like game called "chapitas" using bottle caps and broomsticks. Rodriguez's passion for baseball was so great that he often wore his baseball glove when he was sitting around the house. Some evenings, he even went to bed in his little league uniform. "From the time he was 7, it's been baseball, baseball, baseball," said his mother.

Rodriguez pitched and covered third base for his little league team. During these early years on the diamond, he often found himself playing against Juan Gonzalez, who grew up to become a feared major league slugger — and Rodriguez's teammate on the Texas Rangers for several years. The local baseball field, which Rodriguez still visits regularly, had an uneven infield full of pebbles and an outfield with bare patches in the grass. "It made you always be ready," he recalled. "The ball, it could bounce anywhere. It could hit you right in the face. It taught you to be ready for anything."

It was on that field, surrounded by a rusty fence, graffiti-covered benches, and rickety wooden bleachers, that Rodriguez developed his talent. When he was eight years old, he pitched four no-hitters in one year. "Everybody was afraid to face me. . . . Nobody could hit my fastball," he remembered. "Even when I was little, I could throw a ball. I guess it was my gift." Adults in the neighborhood could tell that he was a special talent as well. "Since Ivan was 9 or 10 years old, in my mind, I knew he was a pro," his father said.

Despite his powerful pitching arm, Rodriguez was persuaded by his father to train as a catcher in little league. Jose Rodriguez feared that his son's short stature would prevent him from becoming a major-league pitcher, since most of them are at least six feet tall. "Everybody is small in the family," Rodriguez explained. "So my father says: 'Let's keep working the catching.'"

Rodriguez embraced the challenge of being a catcher. Big league catchers such as Johnny Bench of the Cincinnati Reds and Lance Parrish of the Detroit Tigers became his heroes, and Rodriguez practiced his catching and batting skills with his father on a regular basis. His father's instructions did not end on the playground either. His parents often sat behind the backstop during games so Rodriguez's father could talk to his son when he was catching or batting. Rodriguez said that his father was ordinarily a very quiet man, but during games he would shout out words of encouragement and advice: "'Think, Ivan! . . . Be aggressive! . . . Play hard!' I wanted to make him happy with me," Rodriguez acknowledged. "My father . . . made me what I am."

An Exciting Prospect

Rodriguez played little league baseball in Vega Baja from age seven to 15. By his early teens he was on the roster of top teams that traveled throughout Latin America. During that time, one of his coaches nicknamed him "Pudge" because of his stocky build. Although Rodriguez disliked the name at first, he grew to accept it.

At age 15, Rodriguez joined the Mickey Mantle League. His performance in this top junior league attracted the attention of several major league scouts, including Luis Rosa and Manny Batista of the Texas Rangers. "He was very smart and aggressive at such a young age," recalled Batista. "It was difficult to find a catcher, at that age, who could do what Ivan did." Rosa offered Rodriguez a contract as a minor-league professional baseball player in July 1988. Although Rodriguez was only 16 years old, Rosa was confident that the player was ready for the challenge. "Pudge was hardnosed, even then," he explained. "He showed leadership at 16 that I'd seen in few kids. He knew where he was going."

Rodriguez admitted that when he left for spring training with the Texas Rangers at the young age of 16, he had very mixed feelings. "I'm still a little kid," he recalled. "My family is crying at the airport, because I leave for the first time alone." Though he was excited about the opportunity ahead, Rodriguez admitted harboring fears and doubts about leaving Puerto Rico. "I don't know how to speak the language at all," he explained. "I don't know how to say yes or no."

EDUCATION

Rodriguez attended Lino Padron Rivera High School in Vega Baja before being discovered by major league scouts. According to his mother, he was very shy in school. "[Ivan was] quiet in the extreme. Even when he was in grade school, teachers literally had to take the words out of his mouth," she said. His favorite subject was math, which came naturally to him, and he has said that he might have pursued a career in accounting if he had not become a professional athlete. Rodriguez left high school before earning his diploma to play baseball, but he often emphasizes the importance of education when he talks to young athletes.

CAREER HIGHLIGHTS

In baseball, some players start their professional careers in the major leagues. But many more start playing for a team in the minor leagues, also called the farm system. The teams in the minor leagues are affiliated with those in the major leagues. There are a variety of minor leagues, which are ranked according to the level of competition. The top or best league is Class AAA (called Triple A), next is Class AA, then Class A, then below that are the rookie leagues. Players hope to move up through the system to a Class AAA team and then to the major leagues.

Rodriguez spent less than three years in the minor leagues before being called up to "The Show" — the major leagues. He started the 1990 season in the Class A Florida State League. His outstanding performance caught the attention of *Baseball America* magazine, which named him the league's best major league prospect. Rodriguez was promoted to Class AA in 1991 and joined the roster of the Tulsa Drillers. Rodriguez immediately earned a reputation for exceptional defensive skills, throwing out 23 of 39 base-stealers in the first two months of the season. "It's unbelievable how hard this kid wants to work," Drillers manager Bobby Jones raved. "Some kids you have to push. But this one comes up begging for it. His attitude and work ethic are outstanding."

On June 20, 1991, Rodriguez was called up to the major leagues to make his debut as a Texas Ranger. Earlier that same day, Rodriguez married Maribel Rivera in Tulsa. In his first major-league appearance, Rodriguez threw out two players who attempted to steal second base and hit a two-run single as the Rangers coasted to a 7-3 victory. "It was a crazy day, in a positive way," Rodriguez recalled. "Getting married was wonderful, and I got a hit in the game. But throwing out two guys, that made the day unforgettable. I really felt proud." The 19-year-old was the youngest athlete in Major League Baseball at the time, a designation he held until the 1993 season. Rodriguez went on to lead all American League catchers in throwing out base-stealers for the 1991 season.

Rodriguez batting for the Texas Rangers in 1991.

Building a Career

Once he reached the big leagues, Rodriguez made it clear that he intended to stick around for a while. By midway through the 1992 campaign — only his second season in Major League Baseball — he was widely regarded as one of the game's fast-rising stars. Tim Kurkjian of *Sports Illustrated* declared that he was "without a doubt, the best-throwing catcher in the American League," and he was named to the American League's All-Star team for the 1992 campaign. He also earned a Gold Glove Award for his exceptional defensive skills at season's end — the first of ten consecutive Gold Gloves for the rocket-armed catcher.

The mid-1990s brought continued success for Rodriguez. He earned the first of six consecutive Silver Slugger Awards (given annually to the best offensive player at each position in each of Major League Baseball's two leagues) in 1994. One year later, he led the Rangers in batting average, total bases, and doubles, and ranked second on the team in hits. His overall performance during the 1995 season prompted the Rangers to name

123

him Player of the Year. At the end of each season, meanwhile, Rodriguez returned to his native Puerto Rico for three months of winter baseball in the Caguas Winter League.

Rodriguez's terrific play made him a fan favorite in Texas. But his popularity also stemmed from his ability to connect with fans. During the final game of the 1995 season with the Texas Rangers, for example, he was introduced to a five-year-old boy with muscular dystrophy, a disease that causes the muscles in the body to weaken and eventually stop working. After talking with the boy for a little while, he invited the youngster to kiss his bat for good luck. Rodriguez then walked out to the plate and hit a home run on the first pitch, a moment he has described as "something out of a movie." As he rounded the bases, he pointed to the boy, who was smiling and clapping from his wheelchair. "After I touched the plate, I ran over to him and hugged him," Rodriguez remembered. "Then I gave him a high five." As Texas Rangers President Tom Schieffer told *Sports Illustrated,* "It's one of those stories that makes you love baseball. I still get a little catch in my throat every time I retell it. I got the feeling that Babe Ruth was up there somewhere and smiling."

> *"I'm really worried about this [contract situation]," Rodriguez admitted to the Texas Rangers. "I don't want to be traded. I love playing here, and I want to stay here. I want to work out a deal."*

During the 1996 campaign, Rodriguez was a key player in the club's rise from mediocrity to playoff contender. As usual, his powerful throwing arm kept opposing base runners from running wild on the base paths. But he also became a bigger force at the plate. His 19 home runs, 86 runs batted in (RBIs), 116 runs scored, and .300 batting average helped lift the Rangers to a 90-72 record and a playoff berth. Unfortunately, Texas lost in the first round of the playoffs to the heavily favored New York Yankees in four games.

The Rangers slumped in 1997, falling to 77-85. But Rodriguez continued to play at a high level. He pounded 20 home runs and registered 77 RBIs to go along with 98 runs scored and a sizzling .313 batting average. He was eligible for free agency at the end of the 1997 season, meaning his contract with the Rangers would end and he would be free to sign with another team. Rumors surfaced that the Major League Baseball Players Association wanted Rodriguez to become a free agent since he would likely command a high salary and thus raise the pay scale for catchers around the league.

With the bases loaded, Rodriguez manages a double play by tagging a runnner out at home and then throwing out the runner at first.

Rodriguez, however, wanted to stay with the Rangers. Much to the surprise of Rangers President Tom Schieffer, Rodriguez appeared at his office door one day and declared his desire to remain with the team. "I'm really worried about this," he confessed. "I don't want to be traded. I love playing here, and I want to stay here. I want to work out a deal." They agreed on a five-year contract worth $42 million.

125

Best Catcher in Baseball

Rodriguez had his best season yet in 1998. His 21 home runs, 91 RBIs, and .321 batting averages were all career bests, and they helped lift Texas to an 88-74 mark and a spot in the playoffs. The season ended in disappointment, though, when team was swept in the first round by the New York Yankees.

In 1999 Rodriguez took his game to such a high level that he became the first catcher in over 20 years to win American League's Most Valuable Player Award from the Baseball Writers Association of America. He earned the honor by throwing out nearly 55 percent of base-stealers—a major league record—and hitting more home runs (35) than any other American League backstop in history. Additionally, he knocked in a career-best 113 runs, including a club record nine RBIs in one game, scored a whopping 116 runs, stole 25 bases himself, and hit at a blazing .332 clip. His exploits enabled the Rangers to compile a 95-67 record and earn a spot in the postseason. But once again, the Yankees dumped Texas in the first round to bring the season to a close for Rodriguez and his teammates.

> «
>
> *Rodriguez received the most votes by fans for the 2000 All-Star game. "It's an honor for me," he remarked. "I never expected in my career that would happen. . . I don't consider myself the best catcher. I just consider myself another player in the game. . . . I'm just trying to do my best."*
>
> »

By the end of the 1999 campaign, Rodriguez had also become the first catcher in major league history to hit at least 20 home runs and steal at least 20 bases in one season. Moreover, he had the highest batting average by a catcher in the American League since 1937. "He dominates his position, offensively and defensively. That's what a great player does," said long-time major league manager Jim Leyland. Fellow superstar Derek Jeter offered a similar assessment: "Pudge has the best arm in baseball, maybe the best arm for a catcher ever. He's quick and he's accurate. The key is being accurate." The media recognized his worth as well. Johnette Howard of *Sports Illustrated,* for example, remarked that Rodriguez's strong work ethic, willingness to learn, and passion for the game, combined with his technical abilities, had made him "the most irreplaceable player in baseball."

Following his record-breaking performance in 1999, Rodriguez's popularity rose to new heights. He received the most votes by fans for the 2000 All-Star game. "It's an honor for me," he remarked. "I never expected in my career that would happen." Rodriguez remained humble, despite the increase in attention. "I don't consider myself the best catcher. I just consider myself another player in the game. . . . I'm just trying to do my best."

Unfortunately, injuries put Rodriguez on the sidelines for extended periods of time in 2000 — and the following two seasons as well. When he was healthy, he remained a top player; in 2000 he hit a career best .347, and the following year he threw out 35 of the 58 players who tried to steal a base against him. But from 2000 to 2002 he missed a total of 176 games, and with their team leader beset by injuries, the Rangers failed to reach 75 victories during any of those years.

The Rangers decided not to re-sign Rodriguez when his contract expired. Team management explained that it simply could not pay a top salary to a player with a recent history of injuries and declining productivity. At the time of his departure, Rodriguez held the ball club's record for all-time at-bats, hits, and doubles. He ranked second in games played, runs, and total bases, and third in home runs and RBIs. It was only fitting, then, that he received multiple standing ovations from the crowd during the last game of the 2002 campaign. Appearing before the home town fans for the final time in a Ranger uniform, Rodriguez hit a home run in the seventh inning, and doubled in the eighth to drive home a run. "[This last day is] something I'll remember . . . for the rest of my career," he affirmed.

Leaving Texas for the Florida Marlins

Rodriguez was offered a one-year, $10-million contract with the Florida Marlins for the 2003 season. Mired in a five-year losing streak, the team's management believed that he could help the team's young pitching staff and give a much-needed boost to the offense. "We saw his injuries, but we didn't see them as major," Florida General Manager Larry Beinfest explained. Rodriguez accepted the offer, and within a matter of weeks he had become a trusted mentor to the team's young hurlers. "He's our captain," said Marlins pitcher Carl Pavano. We look to him for just about everything." Pitcher Chad Fox echoed Pavano, stating: "I've grown to trust him completely. . . . If he believes in me, I believe in myself."

At the start of the season, Rodriguez expressed confidence in his new team. "I think we're going to win a lot of games. I think the 2003 season is going to be the year of the Marlins," he said. His prediction was astoundingly accurate. Aided by his 16 home runs, 85 RBIs, and .297 average, the Marlins

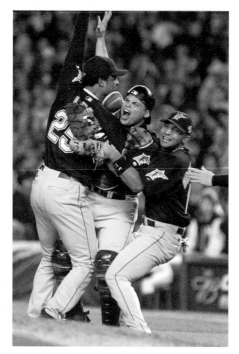

*Rodriguez celebrates with his Florida
Marlins teammates, Derrek Lee (#25)
and Alex Gonzales (#11), after beating
the New York Yankees to win the
2003 World Series.*

marched to a 91-71 regular season record and a playoff birth. Florida then knocked off the San Francisco Giants and the Chicago Cubs (in seven dramatic games) to earn a chance to face the New York Yankees — Rodriguez's old playoff nemesis — in the 2003 World Series. Rodriguez performed at a high level throughout the postseason, contributing 17 RBIs and three home runs. But many analysts claimed that his clubhouse leadership was even more important in helping the Marlins register a stunning triumph over the feared Yankees in six games.

Rodriguez has called the night of the Marlins' World Series victory one of the most memorable of his whole life. After the game, he fulfilled a pledge he had made to his 11-year-old son, Ivan Dereck. "If we win the World Series," Rodriguez had told his son prior to the playoffs, "we're going to walk around the bases, and we're going to get down on our knees and pray." Rodriguez — now a World Series champion — circled the infield of Yankee Stadium with his oldest son, kneeling down before each base. When they reached home plate, they kissed it and knelt together in prayer.

After the season, Rodriguez was named the Most Valuable Player (MVP) of the National League Championship Series and *Baseball Digest*'s 2003 Player of the Year. Through effort and determination, he had proven that despite a few injury-filled years, he still had a lot of baseball left in him. "When you believe in yourself, work hard, and prepare yourself, anything is possible," he declared.

Joining the Detroit Tigers

Armed with a World Series ring and many fond memories, Rodriguez left Florida and signed a four-year contract with the Detroit Tigers prior to the

2004 season. The Tigers had held the worst record in baseball in the 2003 season, but the club's decision to sign the veteran catcher showed players, fans, and sports reporters that it was serious about improving. "Once we got Pudge, we immediately became respectable," manager Alan Trammell said. "He's been the total package."

Once the 2004 season began, Rodriguez displayed leadership ability, drive, and a steadfast commitment to the game. He won his 11th Gold Glove award, the most by any catcher in history, and earned a record-tying seventh Silver Slugger Award on the strength of 19 homers, 86 RBIs, and a sizzling .334 batting average. His performance helped the Tigers win 29 games more than they had a season earlier. Rodriguez also reached several career milestones during the 2004 season. He knocked in his 1000th run, earned his 2,000th career hit, and scored his 1000th career run. Baseball legend Al Kaline expressed pride in seeing Rodriguez meet these milestones as a Detroit Tiger: "To me, he has changed the whole face of this organization. He really has," he said.

——— " ———

"Once we got Pudge, we immediately became respectable," said Detroit Tiger manager Alan Trammell. "He's been the total package."

——— " ———

Heartened by the Tigers' improvement in 2004, many Detroit fans expressed excitement about the approaching 2005 season. But just as the season began, retired major league slugger Jose Canseco, a former Pudge teammate, published a book in which he accused Rodriguez and several other star players of illegal steroid use. Rodriguez denied the allegations. "I'm in shock," he told the press. "[Canseco] is saying things that aren't true, and it hurts me a lot that he would say things like that because I've always had a lot of respect for him, and I've even helped him many times when things weren't going well for him."

Rodriguez had lost 22 pounds prior to the opening of the season. Though he credited the weight loss to a change in diet and exercise, some critics suspected a connection to Canseco's accusation of steroid use. Rodriguez ignored the whispers, but the season was not a happy one for him. In addition to Canseco's allegations, Rodriguez had to deal with a painful divorce and multiple broken bones in his hands. In addition, the Tigers stumbled to a disappointing 71-91 record. Even so, he remained the most feared defensive catcher in the game. By season's end, he had thrown out 35 out of 58 runners who tried to steal a base on him.

Rodriguez shows his superlative fielding skills as he charges out from behind the plate while playing for the Detroit Tigers, 2006.

2006 American League Champions

The 2006 season was one of hope and excitement for the Detroit Tigers. The team roared out of the gate to claim first place in its division. Armed with a stable of hot young pitchers and a tough batting order, the Tigers held the best record in baseball for much of the season. The team stumbled in the home stretch to lose the division crown, but its 95 victories still earned Detroit a spot in the postseason for the first time since 1987.

To the surprise of fans everywhere, the Tigers beat the New York Yankees in the first round of the playoffs, then swept the Oakland Athletics to win the American League Championship. Tiger fans were thrilled, and they talked openly about how sweet it would be to cap a "Cinderella" season with a World Series championship. Their dreams of victory were thwarted, however, when the St. Louis Cardinals defeated the Tigers to clinch the 2006 World Series title.

Rodriguez was disappointed that he fell short in his bid to earn a second World Series champion ring. But he expressed optimism about the future of the team and pride in the role he had played in turning around the Tigers franchise: "I feel very happy, because when I came here three years ago, Mr. Ilitch [the owner of the Tigers] was telling me he was going to put a winning team together. I was the first one to sign here as a free agent and then others came. . . . Now I'm sure there are a lot of players on the market that want to come to Detroit and play. And that for me makes myself very happy."

Rodriguez has admitted, however, that he is not sure if he will end his career in Detroit. He has expressed an interest in returning to Texas to finish his career. "Every player's dream is to start and finish with the same team. I still have a couple of years left in me," he hinted. Wherever he concludes his career, Rodriguez has indicated that he plans to remain in baseball in some capacity for years to come. "I've loved to play this game since I was born," he said. "Baseball is going to be in my blood for life."

> "I feel very happy, because when I came here three years ago, Mr. Ilitch [the owner of the Tigers] was telling me he was going to put a winning team together," said Rodriguez. "I was the first one to sign here as a free agent and then others came. ... Now I'm sure there are a lot of players on the market that want to come to Detroit and play. And that for me makes myself very happy."

MARRIAGE AND FAMILY

Rodriguez wed Maribel Rivera on June 20, 1991 in Tulsa, Okalahoma. Rodriguez and Rivera have three children together: son Ivan Dereck, born June 5, 1992; daughter Amanda Christine, born June 21, 1995; and daughter Ivanna Sofia, born January 12, 2000. Their marriage ended in divorce in 2005.

During the baseball season, Rodriguez resides in Bloomfield Hills, Michigan. His permanent residence is a lavish, nine-bedroom home in Miami, Florida. He has also spent many winters in Rio Piedras, Puerto Rico, an exclusive community south of San Juan.

MAJOR INFLUENCES

Rodriguez has discussed a number of influences on his life and career. Specifically, he has named power pitcher Nolan Ryan and Hall of Fame catcher Johnny Bench as professional inspirations. He also admires legendary outfielder Roberto Clemente, a native of Puerto Rico who helped the poor throughout Latin America before his life was cut short by a tragic plane crash in 1972. In Puerto Rico, Clemente is a symbol of perseverance, leadership, integrity, and charity. "Roberto spent a lot of his time with people. . . . It showed that he really cared. I want to do the same things," Rodriguez said. The Texas Rangers recognized Rodriguez's efforts to follow in Clemente's footsteps, twice naming him Roberto Clemente Man of the Year for his community achievements.

> *"I'm a player who likes to learn every single day because I want to get better," Rodriguez said. "So my father tells me more about what I do wrong than right. The success of my career is because of my father."*

Rodriguez has always identified his father as the most significant influence on his life. "My father was there all the time for me," he emphasized. Jose Rodriguez was his son's first baseball coach, and years later, he continues to offer him guidance in his professional career. Rodriguez appreciates his father's honesty. "I'm a player who likes to learn every single day because I want to get better," he explained. "So my father tells me more about what I do wrong than right. The success of my career is because of my father."

HOBBIES AND OTHER INTERESTS

Rodriguez has admitted that he is addicted to ESPN's "SportsCenter," but he also has various interests outside of the world of professional sports. He reads the Bible on a daily basis and enjoys many different kinds of music, from Elton John to JaRule. He is also a fan of salsa music. His athletic interests other than baseball include swimming, golf, and scuba diving. He also enjoys playing video games and watching professional wrestling.

Rodriguez also devotes a lot of time to the Ivan "Pudge" Rodriguez Foundation, which was founded in 1993. The organization assists the families of children suffering from cancer and other serious diseases. Though the foundation initially focused on helping families in Texas and Puerto Rico, he has recently established a fund at the Children's Hospital of

Michigan to help kids in the Detroit area. "I love kids," Rodriguez said. "I always go into hospitals and talk to kids and try to make them happy." He also has hosted numerous baseball clinics for young athletes to help them learn hitting techniques and fielding skills. "I did the same thing when I was a little kid, seeing older superstars come and do clinics, I was one of those [kids] who sat down and listened to them," he stated. "As long as [the kids] are having fun, and they're smiling and they're happy, that's what I care about."

HONORS AND AWARDS

American League All-Star Team (Major League Baseball): 1992-2001; 2004-06
Rawlings Gold Glove Award: 1992-2001; 2004, 2006
Louisville Silver Slugger Award: 1994-99; 2004
Most Valuable Player Award, American League (Baseball Writers Association of America): 1999
Player of the Year (*Baseball Digest*): 1999; 2003
Most Valuable Player, National League Championship Series: 2003

FURTHER READING

Books

DeMarco, Tony. *Latinos in Baseball: Ivan Rodriguez,* 2000 (juvenile)
Wendel, Tim. *The New Face of Baseball: The One-Hundred Year Rise and Triumph of Latinos in America's Favorite Sport,* 2003
Who's Who in America, 2006

Periodicals

Baseball Digest, July 1, 2001, p.32; Jan. 1, 2004, p.17; Dec. 1, 2004, p.52
Dallas Morning News, Mar. 30, 1997, p.E1; Aug. 21, 2005, p.C6
Detroit Free Press, Feb. 21, 2006, Sports section, p.5; Apr. 6, 2006, Sports section, p.7
Detroit News, July 11, 2006, p.D1; Aug. 15, 2006, p.D5
Sporting News, Jan. 5, 1998, p.56
Sports Illustrated, Aug. 11, 1997, p.40; Feb. 18, 2002, p.58; Oct. 31, 2003, p.12
Sports Illustrated for Kids, Aug. 1997, p.52; July 1999, p.6; June 2003, p.54
Texas Monthly, June 1998, p.114

Online Articles

http://www.puertorico-herald.org
(*Puerto Rico Herald,* "Rangers' Rodriguez Tours Homeland," Mar. 30, 2001, Sports & Entertainment Category Archive, 2001)

Online Databases

Biography Resource Center, 2006, article from *Marquis Who's Who,* 2006

ADDRESS

Ivan "Pudge" Rodriguez
Detroit Tigers
Comerica Park
2100 Woodward Avenue
Detriot, MI 48201

WORLD WIDE WEB SITES

http://detroit.tigers.mlb.com/NASApp/mlb/team/player.jsp?player_id
   =121358
http://sports.espn.go.com/mlb/players/profile?playerID=2523
http://www.pudge/org

Rob Thomas 1965-

American Author, Television Writer, and Producer
Creator of the TV Series "Veronica Mars"

BIRTH

Rob Thomas was born on August 15, 1965, in Sunnyside,
Washington. His parents, Bob and Diana Thomas, were both
teachers. Rob was their only child and he maintained a very
close relationship with his parents throughout his youth.
When Thomas was 10 years old, his family moved from the
Pacific Northwest to Austin, Texas. Two years later they moved

to San Marcos, a small town about 30 miles south of Austin, where his parents operated a sandwich shop.

YOUTH AND EDUCATION

Even as a child, Thomas looked forward to a career as an author. "I've always wanted to be a writer, though the sort of writer I've aspired to be has changed several times," he revealed. "I told my junior high counselor that I was going to be a novelist, but that was when I was bright-eyed and naive."

> *"I've always wanted to be a writer, though the sort of writer I've aspired to be has changed several times," said Thomas. "I told my junior high counselor that I was going to be a novelist, but that was when I was bright-eyed and naive."*

As he grew older, Thomas shifted his sights to journalism. He worked on this goal by writing for his high school paper, and he eventually became the paper's editor. "I'd goof off for three weeks, then my friends who I'd recruited onto staff and I would lock ourselves in and write the entire edition," he remembered. "I have copies of issues in which I've written 14, 15 stories. None of them very good, but I enjoyed seeing my by-line."

Thomas was also an outstanding athlete during high school. He played football, baseball, and basketball, and ran track. Unlike the often-alienated characters he has brought to life in books and on television screens over the years, the adolescent Thomas was a straight arrow who enjoyed his teen years. "I played sports in school, liked my parents, cleaved tenaciously to sobriety, and as uncool as this sounds, enjoyed high school."

After graduating from San Marcos High School in 1983, Thomas attended Texas Christian University. A member of the football team, he played as a sophomore before deciding to leave sports behind and focus on his studies. He won a journalism scholarship and later transferred to the University of Texas at Austin. He received his Bachelor of Arts (BA) degree in history in 1987, as well as his teaching certificate.

EARLY JOBS

Although Thomas had entered college hoping to pursue a career in journalism, by the time he graduated he had his heart set on a life in music. He and some friends had formed a rock band, called Public Bulletin, and by the time he earned his college diploma that group had attracted a modest following. Thomas played bass guitar for the band, but his biggest contribution was a songwriter. He later admitted that the sound of an audience singing along to his lyrics transformed him. "My life goals changed on the spot," he admitted.

For the next several years Thomas devoted most of his free time to music. On most nights and weekends he could be found on stage at one regional venue or another with his band, which was renamed Hey Zeus in 1988 and Black Irish in 1992. His main source of income during this time was a teacher's salary. "I felt like I was a good teacher, but if I hadn't had my own thing outside, some other aspiration, I would have felt like I was selling myself out," he said.

Thomas's teaching career began in 1988 at John Marshall High School in San Antonio, Texas. In 1991 he moved to Austin, Texas, where he taught journalism at Reagan High School. He enjoyed teaching in part because it challenged him to find creative ways to keep his students excited about journalism. He met this goal one semester by entering one of his broadcast journalism classes in a news production competition sponsored by Channel One, a television network broadcast directly into public schools. His students performed so well that Channel One network executives offered Thomas a job. He accepted the position, in part because he wanted a new challenge and in part because he realized that his dreams of musical stardom were fading. He was encouraged in the career change by his family, noting that "the defining moment for me was when my dad sat me down and said I should write."

CAREER HIGHLIGHTS

Thomas moved out to California to join the Channel One staff in 1994. His position was as a liaison between Channel One's educational development department and the schools that subscribed to the service. Unfortunately, Thomas found the job to be boring and tedious. "I felt like this job could have been adequately filled by a zealous coat hanger," he recalled.

Thomas's unhappiness with his new job was made worse by the fact that he was no longer working as a musician. "Suddenly, I had this huge creative void in my life," he recalled. "I wasn't doing anything, so I started [a novel called] *Rats Saw God:* a page a day that filled that hole in my life."

Thomas disciplined himself to write every day, and after 10 months he had completed his first draft. He studied the publishing market and decided to look for an agent. Many writers have great difficulty finding an agent to represent them or a publisher interested in purchasing their manuscripts. But for Thomas, finding an agent and a publisher was easy. "It's funny," the author observed. "I spent nine years beating my head against the wall in this rock 'n' roll band, and it took [only] 10 weeks after I had finished my book to get an agent, and 10 weeks after that to get a book contract." He signed a two-book contract with Simon & Schuster, quit his job at Channel One, and returned to Texas in June 1995 to focus on his writing.

Rats Saw God

Thomas's first novel for young adults, *Rats Saw God*, was published in 1996. It tells the story of Steve York, a California high school senior who has scored high on his college-entrance exams despite a reputation as a flunking-out stoner. A sympathetic counselor challenges him to write a 100-page paper — on any subject — to make up for an English class. Steve decides to write about the experiences that disillusioned him with life and separated him from his father. Steve was a sophomore when his parents divorced and he chose to live with "the Astronaut," as he calls his father. They communicate only through notes and Steve avoids activities he knows his father would find acceptable. Nevertheless, he is a straight-A student until he discovers his girlfriend is having an affair with a teacher. The betrayal devastates Steve, who starts skipping class and smoking pot. But the book ends on a hopeful note, as it becomes clear that the counselor's writing assignment has forced Steve to face the pain in his past, deal with it, and move forward with a greater sense of purpose and maturity.

> "I didn't think I was writing a young-adult book . . . so I didn't alter anything [in **Rats See God**]," Thomas said. "Teenagers don't live profanity-free, sex-free, drug-free lives."

Thomas's novel was notable both for its sense of humor and its perceptive insights into the thoughts and emotions of teenagers. As a reviewer remarked in *St. James Guide to Young Adult Writers*, "[the] protagonists survive in a high school culture tinged by drugs, sex, and profanity, and Thomas accurately captures the adolescent language they utter and philosophies they follow." Thomas recognized that the strong language

and mature themes in his work might raise eyebrows, but he said that "I didn't think I was writing a young-adult book . . . so I didn't alter anything." Besides, he added, "teenagers don't live profanity-free, sex-free, drug-free lives."

139

Rats Saw God found favor with teen readers, librarians, and critics alike. Writing in *School Library Journal,* Joel Shoemaker called the novel a "beautifully crafted, emotionally charged story" with "layers of cynical wit and careful character development. . . Steve's coming-of-age is not a smooth ballistic parabola, but more a series of explosive changes in relationships. These changes suggest to YA readers that, though complex and difficult, it is this weird willingness to establish interconnectedness that makes being human such a trip. This robust first novel is so hip and cool and strong it hurts." *Rats Saw God* won an American Library Association Best Books Award, as well as several other best book citations and state award citations. It also gave Thomas a big jolt of confidence. "When I finished my novel, I felt like I could read the top young-adult novel out there — my favorite, the one I considered a classic — and felt I could match up to that," he said.

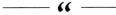

"*For me, coming up with a story idea is the most difficult part of the creative writing process,*" said Thomas. "*If I didn't realize this before, writing a short story collection drove the point home.*"

Slave Day and Other Works

Thomas's second novel, *Slave Day* (1997), also pushed boundaries in addressing issues of prejudice and race. The author uses multiple viewpoints to recount what happens during a school fundraiser, "Slave Day," in which students and teachers in a Texas high school are auctioned off for one day. Keene Davenport, an African-American teen, is offended by Slave Day and tries to organize a boycott. When his protest fails, he ends up "buying" student body president Shawn Greeley, another African American, at the auction. He then has Shawn perform a series of demeaning tasks to show his anger about Slave Day, but the stunt does not turn out as he expects. Other "slaves" and "masters," including a computer geek and the mayor's daughter, an unpopular teacher and a slacker student, and a popular girl and her boyfriend, similarly find their assumptions challenged during the day. "[*Slave Day* is] a cleverly written story that is funny, but that has an underlying serious theme," Judy R. Johnston wrote in *School Library Journal.* "Thomas's quirky humor leads readers and the main characters on a soul-searching experience as themes of equality, racism, feminism, and affirmative action emerge through this intelligently written novel. . . . The final consciousness-raising in the characters' attitudes makes this book a winner. Like Chris Crutcher and Paul Zindel, Thomas has made a distinct contribution to contemporary young adult literature."

Thomas's next book was a short story collection called *Doing Time: Notes from the Undergrad* (1997). Thomas admitted that finishing this book posed a different kind of challenge for him. "For me, coming up with a story idea is the most difficult part of the creative writing process," he noted. "If I didn't realize this before, writing a short story collection drove the point home."

Each story in *Doing Time* follows individual teenagers as they fulfill their high school's community-service requirement. The stories address such serious issues as abuse, poverty, teen pregnancy, and grief. Not only do the

students learn more about these issues, they often learn more about their own feelings. In "Loss of Pet," for instance, a library volunteer makes snap judgments about the library's patrons based on their looks or the books they read. She initially mocks a pretty girl for attending a support group for people who have lost a pet, but finds herself unexpectedly moved by the girl's story. Her reaction forces her to reassess her own attitudes. Other characters in the story collection experience similar moments of self-awareness. "Thomas knows the issues that concern kids, and he does a good job distinguishing each character — from bitchy Teesha, who masks her feelings when the group she is with delivers food to her grandmother, to Dwight, who finds joy in himself and in his Mexican roots when he tutors a school groundskeeper," wrote Stephanie Zvirin in *Booklist*. "Thomas has the language and the emotions down just right — and he never forgets that there's hope."

Thomas returned to the novel form for *Satellite Down* (1998), a work in which he drew on his experiences in television to tell the story of one teen's loss of innocence. Patrick Sheridan is 17 when he wins a spot as a student reporter on an educational satellite television show. He leaves his small Texas town and strict parents to live by himself in Los Angeles. At first he his excited by his job, but he becomes disillusioned when he learns the channel is more interested in his good looks than his reporting skills. He is tempted by alcohol, drugs, sex, and celebrity. But instead of giving in to these temptations, he runs off while in Ireland to explore his family roots. While he finds no easy solutions there, his soul-searching and satirical commentary provide readers with an interesting look into the costs of making your dreams come true. "I know [*Satellite Down* has] a downbeat ending," the author remarked, "but I think there's enough humor and adventure in getting there that it's not a painful ride." A *Kirkus Reviews* critic offered similar thoughts about the novel: "Thomas covers a lot of territory, and Patrick's journeys of the heart are as compelling as his sincere attempts to do the right thing, but readers should be prepared for a raw, ambiguous conclusion."

———— " ————

Thomas only remained on the staff of "Dawson's Creek" for its first season. "It was a fun year for me, because I got to get out of debt with my first TV job, and I learned a ton."

———— " ————

Thomas targeted a slightly younger audience in his 1998 adventure novel *Green Thumb* (1998). This tale concerns award-winning botany student Grady Jacobs, who is excited about earning a spot on a scientific mission to the rainforest. But when team leader Dr. Phillip Carter learns Grady is only 13, he gets stuck with meaningless, dirty jobs. Despite all his chores, Grady discovers that Carter is planting genetically engineered trees that are poisoning the rainforest—a secret the scientist would kill to keep. Grady goes on the run, evading wildlife and Carter's henchmen long enough to expose his crimes. Although it differed in subject matter and intended audience from the author's other novels, *Green Thumb* displayed Thomas's trademark wit, along with a flair for action and adventure. "Readers won't be able to turn the pages fast enough," reviewer John Peter wrote in *Booklist*. "Fans expecting another *Slave Day* or *Rats Saw God* are in for a shock."

Writing for Television and Movies

Thomas's growing reputation as a writer with a knack for reaching teen audiences brought him to the attention of Hollywood. In 1997 he accepted a job as a staff writer for a new television series called "Dawson's Creek." This drama about teens growing up in a small seaside Massachusetts town debuted in 1998 and became an instant hit with teenagers. Some critics complained that the teen characters sounded too articulate for their age. But Thomas said, "I kind of dug writing those kids as though they were college grad students. It was fun and liberating and made for a true sort of writer's show." Although he only remained on the staff of "Dawson's Creek" for its first season, "it was a fun year for me, because I got to get out of debt with my first TV job, and I learned a ton."

That experience would serve Thomas well on his next television job. He had left "Dawson's Creek" because of a fantastic stroke of good fortune: his first pilot script for a television series, called "Cupid," was picked up by ABC to air in the fall of 1998. Two years after moving to Hollywood, executive producer Thomas was now running his own hour-long TV drama. "Cupid" starred

"Dawson's Creek," which starred Katie Holmes, Joshua Jackson, James Van Der Beek, and Michelle Williams.

Jeremy Piven as Trevor Hale, a charismatic mental patient who insists he is the legendary god of love. He claims he has been exiled to earth and must unite 100 couples without using his magic arrows before he can return to Mount Olympus. Psychologist and romance expert Claire Allen, played by Paula Marshall, doesn't believe Trevor but helps him establish a life outside the hospital. Although critics liked the show, ratings were poor and the series was cancelled in February 1999 after 14 episodes.

Thomas was disappointed by the cancellation of "Cupid," but other exciting developments kept him from dwelling on it. In 1999 two films based on Thomas's screenplays were released. One was *Drive Me Crazy*, a teen romantic comedy he adapted from the Todd Strasser novel *How I Created My Perfect Prom Date* (also published as *Girl Gives Birth to Own Prom Date*). Melissa Joan Hart and Adrian Grenier played high school friends from two different social groups who decide to date each other in a bid to make

Thomas adapted the Todd Strasser novel How I Created My Perfect Prom Date *for his screenplay for* Drive Me Crazy, *which starred Adrian Grenier and Melissa Joan Hart.*

other people jealous. Popular with teen audiences, the movie earned a modest $17.8 million at the box office. Thomas's next screenplay to reach the big screen was the small independent film *Fortune Cookie,* about three couples at a Chinese restaurant. The movie was not widely seen, but it earned good reviews.

That same year, Thomas was hired by producer David E. Kelley, creator of such award-winning TV shows as "Chicago Hope," "Ally McBeal," and "The Practice," to work on a new detective show called "Snoops." Thomas left the show before it even aired, however. He had wanted to inject more humor into the series, and "[Kelley] and I didn't get on the same page about what this detective show was going to be," the producer explained. This experience taught him an important lesson: "In fiction I am king of this little world," he noted, "[but in television and film] you are one piece in a committee of people producing this thing and everyone has a voice."

Thomas capped off 1999 by signing a four-year development deal with Fox TV that paid him $8 million. For a guy from small-town Texas, such swift Hollywood success was sometimes overwhelming: "I function pretty well knowing what is going on," he said. "But sometimes, just drifting off to sleep at night, it will hit me and make me seize up, and I'll be terrified."

Thomas's anxiety increased over the next four years. Between 2000 and 2003, he wrote 11 pilot scripts for new television shows that languished in "development hell," never making it to a network (for each series that makes it to television, many others are written and have pilot episodes filmed before being turned down). "There were plenty of things that didn't fly, but there was one that literally broke my heart and gave me true writer's block," he remembered. A network had been very interested in a drama series proposed by Thomas. But the network executive who was most intrigued by the series was fired and Thomas's producing partner died unexpectedly of a heart attack. These setbacks doomed the show, leaving Thomas to try again.

Creating "Veronica Mars"

Thomas's luck finally turned in 2003, when he met with executives for the UPN network to discuss potential projects. During the meeting he mentioned a script he had written for a "teen noir" detective series. "I just started with a vague idea of tackling the noir genre and sticking teenagers into it," the author remembered. "It was one of the first projects I started thinking of visually rather than [in terms of] internalized protagonist dialogue." The image that kept popping up in his imagination was that of a car sitting outside a run-down motel—but the detective sitting in the car is a teenager instead of an adult. Although Thomas first envisioned the character as male, he later decided it would be more interesting to make the character female. The network executives were intrigued, and three days after the meeting they approved production of a pilot episode of the show, called "Veronica Mars." Several months later, the network announced that "Veronica Mars" would debut as a new UPN series in fall 2004.

> **"Unlike a lot of shows, we don't introduce you to the bad guy at the beginning and tell you whodunit," declared Thomas. "We always want Veronica to do something very new and fresh and clever to get to this information, and that's always a challenge."**

The title character, Veronica Mars, is a popular high school girl with a cute boyfriend, loving family, and seemingly charmed life—until her best friend Lilly Kane is murdered. Veronica's father, the local sheriff, accuses Lilly's father of the crime but can't prove his case. Her father loses his job as sheriff, his wife leaves him, and Veronica is ostracized at school. During this time Veronica attends a party and is drugged and raped. The show opens eight months after these events, with Veronica assisting her father in his work as a private detective. Her experiences helping her father show her that harsh truths often lie behind lives that seem perfect on the surface. Played by actress Kristen Bell, Veronica is a pretty girl with a bad attitude—her life has gone so wrong she no longer cares about normal teen problems. "If there's something I've learned in this business," Veronica tells

Kristen Bell (center) and the cast of "Veronica Mars."

viewers, "[it's that] the people you love let you down." Nonetheless, she still has empathy for people around her. She befriends the outsiders at school and feels sorry for the popular kids with hidden problems, even though they have rejected her.

Thomas admitted that "Veronica Mars" had the potential to be a very dark show. "The network was worried about having a teen show where the protagonist has been raped, her friend murdered, her dad a pariah, her mom disappeared," Thomas noted. "How are you going to be able to handle it and have a degree of humor and warmth?" The humor comes from Veronica's comic observations, which display Thomas's trademark wit. These comic bits work well because Thomas and his writers try to integrate them into the story. "I don't want to write setup, punch, setup, punch, where the joke dictates the scene," he explained, "I want to find comedy in which the drama is actually driving the moment in the scene." According to most critics, Thomas succeeded in his goal of blending wit and dramatic tension. As a result, the show quickly gained a devoted fan base.

Viewers can also find warm moments in the series, especially as demonstrated in Veronica's close relationship with her supportive father, played by Enrico Colantoni. She also displays empathy for the people she investigates. In helping her father with his detective work, Veronica sees that many of the people whose lives seem perfect on the surface are battling their own problems. "Providing this peek behind the curtain not only offers a remedy for those teenage snap judgments, it lends the world of 'Veronica Mars' depth and color," wrote TV critic Heather Havrilesky.

Mysteries and Teen Troubles

The first season of "Veronica Mars" was dominated by the mystery of the murder of Lilly Kane, and Thomas rewarded loyal fans at the end of season one by having Veronica solve the mystery. He opened the second season by unveiling another mystery for her to solve — this time a tragic accident in which a school bus drives off a cliff. As the season progressed, Veronica found one clue at a time, giving viewers a chance to solve the mystery at the same time she does. That strategy is deliberate, Thomas said: "Unlike a lot of shows, we don't introduce you to the bad guy at the beginning and tell you whodunit. . . . We always want Veronica to do something very new and fresh and clever to get to this information, and that's always a challenge."

Thomas believes that it is not a coincidence that his greatest success in television has been with a teen character. When asked why he writes for young people, he replied, "It has to do with my affection for teenagers. I like people that age. I find them interesting. It's less about writing how they speak than connecting the thematic truisms of people that age." What makes teens respond to his writing is his honest depiction of their lives, even if that makes for a less-than-happy ending. "I feel compelled to include some bit of truth," Thomas remarked. "It's not truth if our endings are always happy."

Despite its devoted fan base and critical raves, "Veronica Mars" has never been a monster hit in terms of television ratings. Its status for the future became a bit of a mystery in itself in January 2006, when UPN announced that it was merging with the WB Network to form a new television network called the CW. Fans of the show openly worried on Internet fan sites about the show's future. For his part, Thomas projected optimism. He declared that he was hopeful that "Veronica Mars" would not only return for a third season, but that it might run for five or six seasons. "I sort of expect good things to happen," he said. "I don't know where I get it, but I do have a sort of blind optimism." In May 2006 the CW announced that "Veronica Mars" would return for a third season, an announcement that delighted the show's many fans.

Thomas has said that he "would love to write more novels," but his film and television work keeps him so busy—and pays so well—that he is unlikely to return to book writing any time soon. Fortunately, he gets just as much satisfaction out of writing for television. "From childhood on, it's always been writing for me," he noted. "I always have to have some big dream, a creative goal to shoot for, and when I'm writing, I feel like I'm reaching that."

MARRIAGE AND FAMILY

Thomas married Katie Orr, a bookstore manager, in May 2005. Their daughter, Greta Mae, was born that same year. They live in the Hollywood Hills, with neighbors that have included singer Britney Spears and actress Brittany Murphy.

HOBBIES AND OTHER INTERESTS

Thomas loves to read magazines, especially about pop culture, music, and sports. He also enjoys playing basketball and other sports.

SELECTED WRITINGS

Young Adult Fiction

Rats Saw God, 1996
Slave Day, 1997
Doing Time: Notes from the Undergrad, 1997
Satellite Down, 1998
Green Thumb, 1998

Television and Film Scripts

"Dawson's Creek," 1997-98 (TV series; staff writer)
"Cupid," 1998-99 (TV series; creator, executive producer)
Drive Me Crazy, 1999 (movie; script writer)
Fortune Cookie, 1999 (movie; script writer)
"Veronica Mars," 2004- (TV series; creator, executive producer)

HONORS AND AWARDS

Book for the Teen Age (New York Public Library): 1996-97, for *Rats Saw God*
Best Books for Young Adults (American Library Association): 1997, for *Rats Saw God;* 1998, for *Doing Time: Notes from the Undergrad*

FURTHER READING

Books

Hipple, Ted, ed. *Writers for Young Adults,* Supplement 1, 2000
Rockman, Connie. *Eighth Book of Junior Authors & Illustrators,* 2000
Silvey, Anita, ed. *The Essential Guide to Children's Books and Their Creators,* 2002
Something about the Author, Vol. 97, 1998

Periodicals

Austin American-Statesman, June 6, 1996, p.E1; Jan. 16, 1998, p. F1; Aug. 11, 1998, p.E1; Nov. 16, 2004, p.E1
Houston Chronicle, May 10, 2005, sec. STAR, p.1
Mediaweek, May 31, 1999, p.64
Newsday, June 3, 1999, p.B35
Publishers Weekly, Jan. 18, 1999, p.198
San Antonio Express-News, Oct. 14, 1998, p.G1
Texas Monthly, Apr. 1997, p.24
Voice of Youth Advocates, June 1997, p.88

Online Databases

Biography Resource Center Online, 2005, articles from *Authors and Artists for Young Adults,* 1998; *Contemporary Authors Online,* 2005; and *St. James Guide to Young Adult Writers,* 1999

ADDRESS

Rob Thomas
CW Television Network
3300 W. Olive Ave.
Burbank, CA 91505

WORLD WIDE WEB SITES

http://www.robthomasproductions.com
http://www.cwtv.com

Ashley Tisdale 1985-

American Actress and Singer
Star of the Disney Movie *High School Musical* and the
TV Show "The Suite Life of Zack & Cody"

BIRTH

Ashley Michelle Tisdale was born on July 2, 1985, in West
Deal, New Jersey, to Mike and Lisa Tisdale. She has an older
sister, Jennifer, who is also an actress.

YOUTH AND EDUCATION

Tisdale has worked in show business virtually her whole life. "When I was three, I was at the mall with my mom, and this manager came up to us and asked if I wanted to be in commercials," she recalled. This encounter led to a part in a commercial for the national retail chain JC Penney, and from that point forward the youngster knew that she wanted to be an actress. Over the next several years she appeared in more than 100 commercials, including national ads for products including T-Mobile, KFC restaurants, and Sargento cheese.

In 1993, at the age of eight years old, Tisdale landed the role of Cosette in a national touring company version of the famous play *Les Miserables*, based on the novel by the 19th-century French author Victor Hugo. "My mom threw me into some voice lessons to get me prepared for it," she remembered. "It was a really great experience and so I have sung ever since then. I love to sing." Tisdale left the show after two years and joined the cast of the international tour company for the musical *Annie* for a short time. These stage experiences gave her the opportunity to perform at the White House for President Bill Clinton in 1997. "I was a part of Broadway Kids, which was a bunch of kids who were in Broadway shows, and we sang Broadway tunes and met the president," she recalled. "I was so nervous, but it was really fun."

> "I moved from New Jersey to California, so I know what it feels like to be the girl trying to figure it all out," Tisdale explained. "There was this girl in the popular group who was jealous of me, even though I bought my own clothes and car — my parents didn't give them to me. I never told people in school I was an actress. I'm a girl, and acting is my job."

Tisdale's family moved to Valencia, California, when she was in eighth grade. At first, it was a difficult transition. "I moved from New Jersey to California, so I know what it feels like to be the girl trying to figure it all out," she explained. "There was this girl in the popular group who was jealous of me, even though I bought my own clothes and car — my parents didn't give them to me. I never told people in school I was an actress. I'm a girl, and acting is my job."

Tisdale's acting career continued to blossom throughout her high school years. She landed a small role in the 2001 feature film *Donny Darko* and guest starred on numerous television shows, including "The Hughleys," "Charmed," "7th Heaven," "Beverly Hills 90210," "The Amanda Show," and "Boston Public." Yet she claimed that was actually pretty shy during those years. "Believe it or not I was kind of quiet," she said. "I get that side from my dad. My mom is really outgoing."

Tisdale thinks that her shyness may have affected the way other students looked at her. "In high school people would think I was snobby or didn't want to talk to anybody because I was so quiet. But I like being shy!" Being a cheerleader helped her come out of her shell. "My sister was a hardcore cheerleader and I always wanted to follow her," Tisdale explained.

Just a Regular Girl

During Tisdale's adolescence, her parents worked hard to keep show business from dominating her life. "I always had a normal life," she said. "I worked at Wet Seal in the mall and went to a regular school. My dad wanted me to know how long it took to make money and not to take anything for granted." Those long hours of work at the local mall still bring back mixed feelings. "I think it was such a great thing to do," she admitted. "I mean, back then I *hated* it. I had to clean up after shoppers — like scraping gum off the floor — so it was definitely a reality check for me." Tisdale also loved to go horseback riding. She went for the first time when she was eight years old, and eventually developed a strong interest in competitive riding. "I rode mostly when I was 12 or 13, and I did it a lot," she revealed. "I loved doing it."

After graduating from high school, Tisdale decided to take a year off before beginning college. "I really believe in listening to your parents, and my parents are into education," she said. "But I was finished with acting projects and done with school, and I said, 'Dad, I want to take a year off.' So I did." During that time, she worked at the mall and thought a lot about her future. "Really, it was so I could take time to think ahead," she said. "It's good to step back and go, 'What do I like? What do I want?' I knew I wanted to keep acting. So I took it seriously and took classes. I knew I had to work to get what I wanted."

CAREER HIGHLIGHTS

Immediately after high school, Tisdale landed recurring roles on the television series "George Lopez" and "Standing Still." But even as she looked for the part that would firmly establish her name in Hollywood, she encountered doubters. "After I toured with *Les Miserables*, I wanted to come

Tisdale with cast members from "The Suite Life of Zach and Cody" (left to right): Cole Sprouse, Tisdale, Zac Efron, Brenda Song, and Dylan Sprouse.

to California and start doing sitcoms and movies," she remembered. "I met with this agency, and they said, 'She's really sweet, but she'll never make it in Hollywood.'"

Tisdale refused to be discouraged by such comments. "I was like, 'You know *what*? I don't *care* what they say,'" she said. "'I'm gonna go for it and take as many classes as I need.' And it's so funny because years later, this same agent was a manager and knew about me because I was working on so many TV shows. He was like, 'Oh, my gosh, she looks just like Brittany Murphy—she's doing so well,' and my mom was like, 'Yeah, I think *you're* the guy that said that she would never work out here.'"

"The Suite Life of Zack and Cody"

In 2005 Tisdale auditioned for a new Disney project called "The Suite Life of Zack and Cody." This television series revolved around young identical twin brothers living in a luxurious Boston hotel with their mother, a lounge singer. She tested for two roles in the show, London and Maddie, and the producers eventually decided that Tisdale was best suited to play the role

153

of Maddie, the hotel's teenage gift clerk and occasional babysitter for the twins. "I'm really glad that I ended up with Maddie because for fans to first get to know me, I'd rather them look up to this character who is more like me," she said.

Tisdale was very excited to appear on a Disney show. "I love Disney because I'm really, really young still," she asserted. "I never really felt comfortable, even before I was on Disney, doing any type of roles that are really mature. I always wanted to work for Disney my whole life." She admitted that her agent had doubts about taking the role. "My agent did not want me at the Disney channel because I'm older," she said. "But, honestly, I'm not ready for older roles yet, or even the things older girls do. I really am young! All my friends are 16 and 17. I don't go clubbing. I don't drink. I'd much rather have a sleepover or go bowling with girlfriends. I guess you could say I'm not very worldly yet."

> "The Suite Life of Zack and Cody" quickly became one of the Disney Channel's most popular shows. According to Tisdale, it also was a wonderful place to work. "We are like a huge family, from the beginning, from the pilot," she said.

When the executives at the Disney Channel decided to add "The Suite Life of Zack and Cody" to their lineup in 2005, the show's producers asked Tisdale to cut and straighten her hair and dye it from her natural brunette to blonde. She agreed to it, but had mixed feelings about the change. "They cut off seven inches and dyed it blonde and began to straighten it twice a week," she recalled. "As it came along, I started to feel doubt, like, 'Oh, did they not like me or my look before?'" Tisdale's doubts about the change intensified when some fans complained that she was trying to imitate another young star, Hilary Duff. "Some of the fans have said, 'Oh, she's just trying to be Hilary Duff,' but me dyeing it blonde, cutting it short, and straightening it — that wasn't even my *choice*," she declared. "That's just for a character. So it's hurtful when people perceive me as trying to be somebody else."

"The Suite Life of Zack and Cody" quickly became one of the Disney Channel's most popular shows. According to Tisdale, it also was a wonderful place to work. "We are like a huge family, from the beginning, from the pilot," she said. "We only had like a week to shoot the pilot — like we bonded. It was just amazing." In addition to her friends on the show, Tisdale has established friendships with several other actresses affiliated

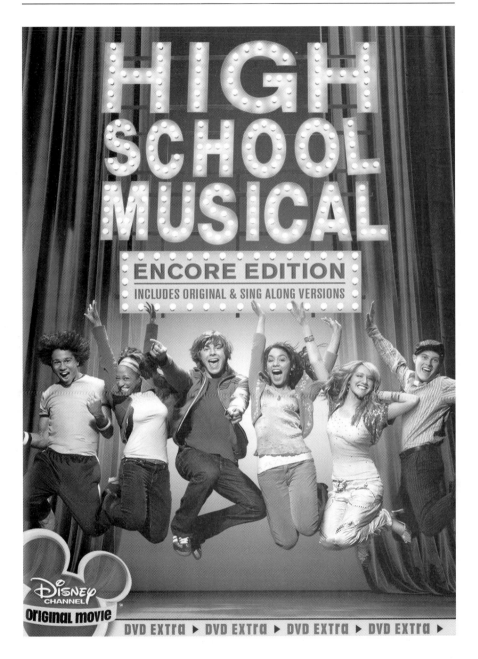

with the Disney Channel, including Raven Symone, and the sister team of Aly and A.J. "Once you're in the business, you kind of just get to know everybody," she explained. "You audition with these people, you're friends with these people. I always stay friends with everybody."

Tisdale has admitted that it is sometimes easier to maintain friendships with fellow actors because they understand the pressures of the profession. "All my friends are in the business because it's kind of hard," she said. "A lot of people were jealous and didn't understand. I just got to know all these people. It's kind of cool that we ended up on the same channel."

High School Musical

During the summer hiatus of "The Suite Life of Zack and Cody," Tisdale was determined to keep busy. "I love working, when I'm not working I get so bored," she said. "I was like, what am I going to do for a couple months? I don't know what I'm going to do. So for two weeks on hiatus I was already bored. . . . And suddenly *High School Musical* came around and I went to audition for it."

—— " ——

"It doesn't really matter what everybody else thinks — it's just what makes you happy. Performing is what makes **me** *happy, I couldn't care less if people don't like it — that's fine. I love proving people wrong."*

—— " ——

High School Musical was a Disney original film project. Despite her relationship with the studio, Tisdale still had to audition for a role in the film. "A lot of people think [I landed a part in the movie] because I'm on Disney, but I had to go on audition, and callback," she pointed out. "It wasn't like it was handed to me at all. I had to go in there and get it myself."

In *High School Musical*, Tisdale plays the role of Sharpay Evans, a popular but mean girl who plots against two students, Troy and Gabrielle, when they get the lead roles in the school play. Jealous of the talented newcomers, Sharpay and her twin brother Ryan plot to stop Troy and Gabrielle from performing in the musical. "Girls get mean when they feel threatened," Tisdale observed. "Sharpay's feet get stepped on, so she gets vicious. Mean girls are the same way. I think they're very insecure. They look like they have it all together, but it's a mask."

Tisdale did find an aspect of the character that she liked, though. "[The] thing I can relate to is, she has this *drive* — it doesn't matter if people don't think she's the best dancer or performer, because *she* thinks she is," she said. "It doesn't really matter what everybody else thinks — it's just what makes you happy. Performing is what makes *me* happy, I couldn't care less if people don't like it — that's fine. I love proving people wrong."

Scenes from
High School Musical.

To prepare for the role, Tisdale trained very hard with other members of the cast. "I knew when I got the role it was going to be a challenge, but I love challenges," she said. "We had a 'boot camp.' It was like two weeks of dance rehearsal. I'm not really coordinated very well." Tisdale, though, believes that these rehearsals created a sense of warmth and fun on the set that carried over on the screen. "Kenny Ortega [the director] would put together Teen Club Night . . . having a little club scene just for us and the dancers," said Tisdale. "That was really cool and I think that's why the experience was so amazing and maybe why this movie has become so successful because they saw how much fun we were having. . . . I think it showed up on screen that we all were having a blast. It looked like a huge party."

High School Musical proved to be a tremendous success for the Disney Channel. It quickly became its highest-rated show ever—almost 8 million people tuned in for its TV debut—and won an Emmy for Outstanding Children's Program. It also won a 2006 Teen Choice Award for Choice Comedy/Musical Program. Moreover, the soundtrack to the movie was one of the best-selling CDs of 2006. Ashley freely admitted that the film's popularity caught her by surprise. "I knew it was really good because when we were filming we could just tell it was really good," she claimed. "We had a lot of support from Disney and we had a great director and we trusted him and we knew it was going to be good, but we never knew it was going to be this good. It was really awesome to hear the ratings and the album kind of came from left field, like we did not know it was going to be that successful."

Future Plans

Reflecting on her own recent accomplishments, Ashley is happy that her career has evolved the way it has. "You know, I think everybody has their own path," she said. "I'm glad I took this road, where I was struggling at first, because now I don't take anything for granted."

Meanwhile, Tisdale has ambitious plans for the future. She will once again play the role of Sharpay in a sequel to *High School Musical,* which is planned for release in 2007. "I probably want to do some more movies," she added. "But I always, always, want to have a sitcom. I would love to always have a TV show and then do movies on the side as well. My goal is to win an Emmy one day, not an Oscar."

Tisdale is also planning for a career in music. In the summer 2006 of she signed with Warner Brother Records to record a solo album. "It will be a growing part of my life," she said. "After we do the sequel [to *High School Musical*], I want to write my music. It'll be like the growing stage."

SELECTED CREDITS

Les Miserables, 1993-95 (stage play)
"The Suite Life of Zack and Cody," 2005- (TV series)
High School Musical, 2006 (TV movie)

FURTHER READING

Periodicals

American Cheerleader, Feb. 2006, p.27
Bop, June-July 2006, p.62
Girls' Life, Aug.-Sep. 2006, pp.44
Newsday, Mar. 1, 2006, p.C14
People, Apr. 10, 2006, p.95
Seventeen, July 2006, p.104
Teen, Summer 2006, p.24
Tiger Beat, June 2006, p.10

Online Articles

http://www.teacher.scholastic.com/scholasticnews/mtm/starspotlight.asp?
   sf=tisdale
   (*Scholastic News Online,* "Star Spotlight: Ashley Tisdale," undated)
http://www.thestarscoop.com/ashley-tisdale.php
   (*Starscoop.com,* "Ashley Tisdale," undated)
http://www.timeforkids.com/TFK/kidscoops/story/0,14989,1169108,00.html
   (*TimeforKids.com,* "The Scoop on *High School Musical,*" Mar. 2, 2006)

Online Databases

Biography Resource Center Online, 2006

ADDRESS

Ashley Tisdale
c/o Disney Channel
3800 West. Alameda Avenue
Burbank, CA 91505

WORLD WIDE WEB SITES

http://www.ashleytisdale.com
http://www.disney.go.com/disneychannel

Photo and Illustration Credits

Drake Bell/Photos: Chris Cuffaro/Nickelodeon (pp. 9, 13 middle, 15, front cover); Nickelodeon (p. 13 top); copyright © 2005 Paramount Pictures (p. 13 bottom).

Taylor Crabtree/Photos: courtesy Taylor Crabtree (pp. 18, 21).

Roger Federer/Photos: Rabih Moghrabi/AFP/Getty Images (p. 25); Clive Brunskill/Getty Images (pp. 28, 31); Timothy A. Clary/AFP/Getty Images (p. 33); Kevin Lamarque/Reuters/Landov (p. 35).

June Foray/Photos: David Livingston/Getty Images (p. 39); copyright © Walt Disney Pictures*Photofest (p. 42 top); copyright © CBS*Photofest (p. 42 middle); copyright © Warner Bros.*Photofest (p. 42 bottom); copyright © ABC*Photofest (p. 45).

Alicia Keys/Photos: AP Images (p. 49); Frank Micelotta/Getty Images (p. 53); Gary Hershon/Reuters/Landov (p. 59). CD covers: THE DIARY OF ALICIA KEYS (J Records) copyright © 2006 Sony Music Entertainment, Inc.; SONGS IN A MINOR (p) 2001 and copyright © 2002 J Records LLC. BMG Company/BMG Entertainment.

Cheyenne Kimball/Photos: courtesy of MTV (p. 64); Evan Agostini/Getty Images (p. 71). CD cover: THE DAY HAS COME (Epic Records) copyright © 2006 Sony Music Entertainment, Inc.

Barack Obama/Photos: courtesy office of Sen. Barack Obama (p. 74, front cover); Simon Maina/AFP/Getty Images (p. 80); Steve Liss/Time Life Pictures/Getty Images (p. 83); AP Images (p. 85); Robyn Beck/AFP/Getty Images (p. 87); Mark Wilson/Getty Images (p. 89). Cover: DREAMS FROM MY FATHER (Three Rivers Press/Crown Publishing Group) copyright © 1995, 2004 by Barack Obama.

Soledad O'Brien/Photos: courtesy of CNN (p. 93, 100, 102, front cover); AP Images (p. 97).

Skip Palenik/Photos: courtesy of Microtrace (p. 106, 108, 110, 113, 116).

Ivan "Pudge" Rodriguez/Photos: Steve Grayson/WireImage.com (p. 119); Louis DeLuca/MLB/Getty Images (p. 123); AP Images (p. 125); Al Bello/Getty Images (p. 128); Ron Vesely/MLB/Getty Images (p. 130).

Rob Thomas/Photos: Kevin Winter/Getty Images (p. 135); copyright © Warner Bros. (p. 143); copyright © 1999 Twentieth Century Fox (p. 144); Robert Voets/UPN. Copyright © 2005 CBS Broadcasting Inc. All rights reserved (p. 146). Covers: RATS SAW GOD copyright © 1996 by Rob Thomas. Cover copyright © 1996 by Simon & Schuster; SLAVE DAY (Aladdin/Simon & Schuster) copyright © 1997 by Rob Thomas. Cover photo copyright © 1998 by Hirotsugo Nushioka/Photonica.

Ashley Tisdale/Photos: copyright © Disney. All rights reserved (pp. 150, 153, 157, front cover). DVD cover: HIGH SCHOOL MUSICAL: ENCORE EDITION copyright © Disney. All rights reserved.

Cumulative Names Index

This cumulative index includes the names of all individuals profiled in *Biography Today* since the debut of the series in 1992.

For cumulative general, places of birth, and birthday indexes, please see biographytoday.com.

For cumulative general, places of birth, and birthday indexes, please see biographytoday.com.

Biography Today

General Series

Biography Today **General Series** includes a unique combination of current biographical profiles that teachers and librarians — and the readers themselves — tell us are most appealing. The **General Series** is available as a 3-issue subscription; hardcover annual cumulation; or subscription plus cumulation.

Within the **General Series**, your readers will find a variety of sketches about:

- Authors
- Musicians
- Political leaders
- Sports figures
- Movie actresses & actors
- Cartoonists
- Scientists
- Astronauts
- TV personalities
- and the movers & shakers in many other fields!

ONE-YEAR SUBSCRIPTION

- 3 softcover issues, 6" x 9"
- Published in January, April, and September
- 1-year subscription, list price $62. **School and library price $60**
- 150 pages per issue
- 10 profiles per issue
- Contact sources for additional information
- Cumulative Names Index

HARDBOUND ANNUAL CUMULATION

- Sturdy 6" x 9" hardbound volume
- Published in December
- List price $69. **School and library price $62 per volume**
- 450 pages per volume
- 30 profiles — includes all profiles found in softcover issues for that calendar year
- Cumulative General Index, Places of Birth Index, and Birthday Index

SUBSCRIPTION AND CUMULATION COMBINATION

- $99 for 3 softcover issues plus the hardbound volume

For Cumulative General, Places of Birth, and Birthday Indexes, please see www.biographytoday.com.

"Biography Today will be useful in elementary and middle school libraries and in public library children's collections where there is a need for biographies of current personalities. High schools serving reluctant readers may also want to consider a subscription."
— *Booklist,* American Library Association

"Highly recommended for the young adult audience. Readers will delight in the accessible, energetic, tell-all style; teachers, librarians, and parents will welcome the clever format [and] intelligent and informative text. It should prove especially useful in motivating 'reluctant' readers or literate nonreaders."
— *MultiCultural Review*

"Written in a friendly, almost chatty tone, the profiles offer quick, objective information. While coverage of current figures makes *Biography Today* a useful reference tool, an appealing format and wide scope make it a fun resource to browse." — *School Library Journal*

"The best source for current information at a level kids can understand."
— Kelly Bryant, School Librarian, Carlton, OR

"Easy for kids to read. We love it! Don't want to be without it."
— Lynn McWhirter, School Librarian, Rockford, IL